Defining Christianity

Defining Christianity

Scott Basham

Table of Contents

PREFACE

If someone visits a Christian church, what will they learn in that hour? Will they discover what Christianity is?

If you were a member of that church, and you wanted that visitor to understand what Christianity is, what would you do? Is there something you could give the visitor to help explain it to them?

In response to those questions, this book was written. The intention of this book is to help anyone who has questions about the Christian faith to get a quick but comprehensive view of what Christianity is.

Additionally, there are important concepts included to inform and challenge those who have been a Christian for a long time. Here are a few unsolicited quotes from early reviewers, all longtime Christians:

"Definitely inspired me to be a better Christian. I think my favorite section was actually 'What is Sin.' "

"My favorite thing, apart from the knowledge it teaches chapter-by-chapter, is the tone with which it teaches. Within the first two chapters, walls come down as people realize that the author is aware of their preconceived notions and willing to have a fair and reasonable discussion."

"The simplest explanation of the most complex biblical topics."

"I love the practicality of it."

"After reading the book I left with a renewed understanding of who God is."

"Defining Christianity left me feeling thankful, convicted, encouraged and deeply, deeply loved."

This book can be read quickly, but it also provides opportunity to explore the different topics in depth. Church classes could use this as material so members can study the topics, and discuss in groups what they learned.

Everything mentioned here is based on the Bible, because that is our standard—for it to have real value, it must align with what the Bible says.

INTRODUCTION

Growing up, you learned about God. Whether your parents, teachers, and friends believed in God or not, they taught you about God. Whether anyone on TV, in the movies, or in books believed in God, they taught you about God. Take all that teaching, bundle it together over the years, and you now have your view of who God is.

But is it correct?

We tend to trust all these sources of information. We trusted our parents, we trusted our teachers, we trusted what we heard on TV, until we saw a crack in their armor, and something we learned from them wasn't quite right.

My wife grew up eating something her dad called "sconions." She called them that as well. She didn't learn until she was an adult that the rest of the world calls them "scallions."

What is your view of God now? I expect much of it is a pretty good picture of who God is. And then, maybe, some of it is not. How do you know? What is true about God? Who is He, and what does He want?

The good thing is we have a completely perfect and reliable document that can give us the truth, that can answer these questions for us—the Bible.

The challenge as you become a Christian and grow in your relationship with God, is to develop a proper view of Him. You need to leave behind all you were taught about God that is off-track, and to shape and solidify and perfect your view of Him based on the Bible.

Why should we trust the Bible? I believe God has a very specific message for us, and I believe He made sure that message was available to us. As the Bible was put together by humans, God was involved in every step of the way, making sure when it was complete, it said what He wanted it to say. When we read the Bible, we are getting a direct look into God.

Everything from God is truth. He is the creator of the Universe and all that is in it, so He is truth. Many people over the centuries have sought truth, and the amazing thing is we have the answer to those questions, direct from God, in the Bible.

Here is a critical point in understanding God: the Bible is from God, and it tells us about Him, and His son Jesus. It tells us about us, and about eternity. It contains the answers for the deepest of all mankind's questions, and it is the standard against which everything else is measured.

Let's explore what the Bible has to tell us. Let's learn together about God, about Jesus, about the Holy Spirit, and about sin, life, death, heaven, hell, and eternity. Let's carefully examine the words of Scripture, comparing them to the view of God we have formed over the many years. Let's get as correct a picture of the heavenly things as we can get.

Our relationship with God will be strengthened as we get a better understanding of who He is.

God is here. We have His voice, His words to us.

Let's draw close to God, together.

HOW TO READ THIS BOOK

This book is divided into chapters according to important themes and topics found in the Bible. It is encouraged for you to read through it, so you can get a broad understanding of what is in the Scriptures. But each chapter is self-contained, and can be read independent of the others.

Throughout the book, you will see verse references next to the text. These references are listed with each concept so as you read the book, you can do research, and see where in the Bible it is found. You'll find the text of the verse references at the end of each chapter, in the same order the verse references are listed in the chapter. The verse text is taken from the English Standard Version of the Bible.

Since the topics are intentionally only presented as overviews, you can select chapters of particular interest and research them in more detail on your own, gaining a deeper insight into them.

If you disagree with any content in this book, review the associated verse references, and search the Bible. Every effort was made for the Bible to be the source of the words here. My prayer is every word presented here gives the truths found in the Bible. And in so doing, may God bless these words in your life.

Defining Christianity

1

TELL ME ABOUT THE BIBLE

2 Tim. 3:16
Rev. 1:19

2 Pet. 1:21

John 17:17
Ps. 119:151

God gave us the Bible. The Bible is not just a collection of written works by various authors over the years—it is a message God planned and coordinated so it would get to us. It is God's communication to us. This is important to understand. We need to know God is the author and constructor of the Bible. He worked with people via the Holy Spirit to say what He wanted to say.

If anyone wonders why we believe the entire Bible is true, we can spout information about the authors, about canon, about continuity, and about how the early church accepted its authority. But the primary reason is if God had a message to get to us, He'd make sure it got to us, that it said what He wanted it to say, that it was accurate, and that it remained untainted over the years. Because we believe this is God's handiwork, we can trust and believe it is truth.

Let's look at what makes up the Bible.

A testament is a statement of truth, and the Bible contains the testament about events before Jesus, called the Old Testament, and the testament about events from Jesus' birth, called the New Testament. There are sixty-six books in the Bible, written by more than forty authors. It was written in three languages—Hebrew, Aramaic, and Greek, over the span of about 1500 years. There is a lot of personality of the individuals in the books, with some being more elegant in their prose than others. The Bible contains history, laws, and principles. Originally, each book was written without chapters and verses, but for readability and structure, they were added.

The Bible has been translated from the original languages into more than 2,000 languages. It has been translated into English many times, each time as either a paraphrase or a translation of the Bible. A paraphrase attempts to give the concepts without necessarily matching the exact text. A translation is intended to be a word-for-word version, produced to match exactly what the author wrote. The first English translation was finished in A.D. 1382 by John Wycliffe. The most read and most famous translation is the King James Bible, supervised by the Church of England, and written by over forty-seven scholars. Other commonly used and respected translations include New International Version, New King James Version, New Living Translation, English Standard Version, and New American Standard.

As you read the Bible, pay attention to how passages fit into the overarching theme of the Bible—God's love for mankind and His provision of forgiveness through Jesus Christ. Throughout the Old Testament, the Bible looks forward to what Jesus would do for mankind, and throughout the New Testament, it points to what Jesus did and is yet to do. | Isa. 55:7
Luke 15:10
John 14:6
Isa. 9:6

Should we read the Bible? Of course. It is God's carefully crafted word to us, conveying what He wanted us to know about Himself and everything related to Him. It answers the fundamental questions of who are we, where do we come from, where do we go when we die, and what is the meaning of life.

Yes, we should read it. And study it, and meditate on it, and memorize it. This is the best way to get to know God, and how to live with Him. | Ps. 119:148
Ps. 119:11

Verses from this section:

2 Timothy 3:16 All Scripture is breathed out by God and profitable for teaching, for reproof, for correction, and for training in righteousness,

Revelation 1:19 Write therefore the things that you have seen, those that are and those that are to take place after this.

2 Peter 1:21 For no prophecy was ever produced by the will of man, but men spoke from God as they were carried along by the Holy Spirit.

John 17:17 Sanctify them in the truth; your word is truth.

Psalm 119:151 But you are near, O Lord, and all your commandments are true.

Isaiah 55:7 let the wicked forsake his way, and the unrighteous man his thoughts; let him return to the Lord, that he may have compassion on him, and to our God, for he will abundantly pardon.

Luke 15:10 Just so, I tell you, there is joy before the angels of God over one sinner who repents."

John 14:6 Jesus said to him, "I am the way, and the truth, and the life. No one comes to the Father except through me.

Isaiah 9:6 For to us a child is born, to us a son is given; and the government shall be upon his shoulder, and his name shall be called Wonderful Counselor, Mighty God, Everlasting Father, Prince of Peace.

Psalm 119:148 My eyes are awake before the watches of the night, that I may meditate on your promise.

Psalm 119:11 I have stored up your word in my heart, that I might not sin against you.

2

WHO IS GOD?

If you are married, how much did you know about your spouse after you'd known him or her for a month? When you got engaged? A month after you were married? And now? I'm sure there are huge differences.

When we meet a person, we learn a lot about them. We get to see all the basics of who this person is—their family, their work, their play. But with more time, we have the chance to get a deeper look.

Like people, we can learn a lot about God. And then with more time, we're able to get a deeper look.

Let's take a look at the basics of who God is.

God created the Universe. He designed all of life. Gen. 1:1

God was around before our Universe. When it was time, He created all things. 2 Kin.gs 19:15

God is big, really big. Study this Universe He created. Our sun is just one star in the Milky Way Galaxy, which is just one of billions of galaxies. God is really big. Job 22:12

God is powerful. The forces of the Universe are so strong they are practically beyond our imagination. For example, a black hole is so strong that nothing, even light, cannot escape from its pull. Rom. 8:38-39

God has a perfect plan for everything. Study how the earth rotates around the sun, in perfect balance, to softly give us the four seasons of the year without extreme climates that would not allow life. Ps. 40:5

God works in extreme details. In addition to the vastness of the Universe, He also worked out the minute details of how atoms interact, and how molecules are formed.

He designed the human body to see. I find it amazing how the eye changes light patterns to electrical signals which tell the brain what something looks like. And, He made us to hear, to touch, to replenish with oxygen and Psa. 139:14

food, to think, etc. God figured out how to get all that to work together in a marvelous way.

God can control and adjust anything to His choosing. If He chooses, He can move mountains. He can bring someone back to life, which means getting all those amazing features of the human body to start working again when they've been broken beyond repair. He can make metal axes float. He can make donkeys talk. He can alter weather patterns.

It is critical to understand—these are acts of God which we call miracles. While God created nature and set things in motion (e.g. you plant a seed and watch it grow into a tree), God sometimes intervenes with miracles— events that would not occur naturally. You must realize it was God who designed and formed the Universe and everything in it. So certainly, God has the power to alter things after the creation was complete.

Please don't try to require natural means for events that truly are miracles, things that would not have happened without God using His power to alter things. When the Red Sea parted, it was not some weird storm— it was God stepping in—it would not have happened if He had not intervened. If you can accept God created the Universe, accept that the parting of the Red Sea was a miracle. Don't limit God. When you hear about a miracle, know something happened outside of what physics controls.

God has a view into all of time. He knows all that has taken place in history, and knows and controls all that will take place in the future.

God is everywhere. A tree does not fall in the woods without Him knowing. He knows of every bird that leaves its nest, of every fish in the sea, of every bolt of lightning, and of every drop of rain or snow that trickles down from the clouds.

God never tires. He is always alert and available and ready to help when we come to Him.

We limit God because we humanize Him. God is much bigger than we envision Him to be. Develop a huge image of God. Because He is huge.

If all that is not amazing enough, beyond all those things, the most remarkable aspect of God, is who He is

1 Kings
17:22
2 Kings 6:6
Num. 22:28
Jon. 1:12,15

Exod. 34:10

Joel 3:17

Matt. 10:30

Isa. 40:28

in His character, in His nature, in His personal make-up, in the attributes of His personality.

To start with, He watches every person, and every little aspect of each person's life. He has great, great passion for each person. He loves them beyond measure. This is a love so deep it goes beyond our understanding. This love is the love He has for you. | Rom. 8:38-39

As a result of His love, He responds to those who seek Him, who want Him in their lives. Those who make the effort to have a heart for God see that He is:

- Gracious—He gives us what we don't deserve or earn | 1 Cor. 15:10
- Merciful—He doesn't punish us in the way we *do* deserve | Eph. 2:4
- Patient—He continuously hopes the best for us despite the many times we let Him down | 2 Pet. 3:9
- Kind—He always treats us softly | Rom. 2:4
- Joyful—we don't often associate God with this attribute, but God's experiences are fun, rich, and full | Neh. 12:43
- Faithful—God never changes, and can always be trusted—He will be there for you | Deut. 32:4
- Peaceful—God loves harmony, and He is so full of peace we almost can't imagine it | Phil. 4:7
- Good—Naturally, God is good, because God defines goodness, and well, being good is being like God | Ps. 31:19
- Controlled—He does nothing without thought and planning—it is always without regret | Ps. 33:11

God is perfect. And as a result, God also has extremely high standards for us: | Matt. 5:48

- He gets angry when we ignore or reject Him | Josh. 23:16
- He demands perfection from us (thankfully, He sees us through the salvation in Christ)
- God is jealous—He wants our love, and wants the love we have for Him to be greater than our | Exod. 34:14

love for any other person or thing

How is God both so loving and demanding? It's not hard to see. We are the same with our children. We love them like crazy but want them to be the best they can be. God, who is the Father, in His perfection, does that to perfection—complete love, and complete expectation for us to be the best. We do fail often, but if He sees a heart for Him, His mercy is also complete.

Ps. 47:7 God is the ruler of the Universe, of all things. He is King, but far more. We are to worship Him, praise Him, honor Him in every way, not because of His position, but because of who He is.

Ps. 7:17 This is a little hard to understand, because our impression of anyone who wants praise is arrogant. Not God. He wants praise because it is totally right. He is the only one fully and completely worthy of praise.

And yet, as high as God is, He wants the best for you. This is His passion. He loves you, and carefully crafts all of life for your success.

Verses from this section:

Genesis 1:1 In the beginning, God created the heavens and the earth.

2 Kings 19:15 And Hezekiah prayed before the Lord and said: "O Lord, the God of Israel, enthroned above the cherubim, you are the God, you alone, of all the kingdoms of the earth; you have made heaven and earth.

Job 22:12 "Is not God high in the heavens? See the highest stars, how lofty they are!

Romans 8:38-39 For I am sure that neither death nor life, nor angels nor rulers, nor things present nor things to come, nor powers, nor height nor depth, nor anything else in all creation, will be able to separate us from the love of God in Christ Jesus our Lord.

Psalm 40:5 You have multiplied, O Lord my God, your wondrous deeds and your thoughts toward us; none can compare with you! I will proclaim and tell of them, yet they are more than can be told.

Psalm 139:14 I praise you, for I am fearfully and wonderfully made. Wonderful are your works; my soul knows it very well.

1 Kings 17:22 And the LORD listened to the voice of Elijah. And the life of the child came into him again, and he revived.

2 Kings 6:6 Then the man of God said, "Where did it fall?" When he showed him the place, he cut off a stick and threw it in there and made the iron float.

Numbers 22:28 Then the Lord opened the mouth of the donkey, and she said to Balaam, "What have I done to you, that you have struck me these three times?"

Jonah 1:12 He said to them, "Pick me up and hurl me into the sea; then the sea will quiet down for you, for I know it is because of me that this great tempest has come upon you."

Jonah 1:15 So they picked up Jonah and hurled him into the sea, and the sea ceased from its raging.

Exodus 34:10 And he said, "Behold, I am making a covenant. Before all your people I will do marvels, such as have not been created in all the earth or in any nation. And all the people among whom you are shall see the work of the Lord, for it is an awesome thing that I will do with you.

Joel 3:17 "So you shall know that I am the Lord your God, who dwells in Zion, my holy mountain. And Jerusalem shall be holy, and strangers shall never again pass through it."

Matthew 10:30 But even the hairs of your head are all numbered.

Isaiah 40:28 Have you not known? Have you not heard? The Lord is the everlasting God, the Creator of the ends of the earth. He does not faint or grow weary; his understanding is unsearchable.

Romans 8:38-39 For I am sure that neither death nor life, nor angels nor rulers, nor things present nor things to come, nor powers, nor height nor depth, nor anything else in all creation, will be able to separate us from the love of God in Christ Jesus our Lord.

1 Corinthians 15:10 But by the grace of God I am what I am, and his grace toward me was not in vain. On the contrary, I worked harder than any of them, though it was not I, but the grace of God that is with me.

Ephesians 2:4 But God, being rich in mercy, because of the great love with which he loved us,

2 Peter 3:9 The Lord is not slow to fulfill his promise as some count slowness, but is patient toward you, not wishing that any should perish, but that all should reach repentance.

Romans 2:4 Or do you presume on the riches of his kindness and forbearance and patience, not knowing that God's kindness is meant to lead you to repentance?

Nehemiah 12:43 And they offered great sacrifices that day and rejoiced, for God had made them rejoice with great joy; the women and children also rejoiced. And the joy of Jerusalem was heard far away.

Deuteronomy 32:4 "The Rock, his work is perfect, for all his ways are justice. A God of faithfulness and without iniquity, just and upright is he.

Philippians 4:7 And the peace of God, which surpasses all understanding, will guard your hearts and your minds in Christ Jesus.

Psalm 31:19 Oh, how abundant is your goodness, which you have stored up for those who fear you and worked for those who take refuge in you, in the sight of the children of mankind!

Psalm 33:11 The counsel of the Lord stands forever, the plans of his heart to all generations.

Matthew 5:48 You therefore must be perfect, as your heavenly Father is perfect.

Joshua 23:16 if you transgress the covenant of the Lord your God, which he commanded you, and go and serve other gods and bow down to them. Then the anger of the Lord will be kindled against you, and you shall perish quickly from off the good land that he has given to you."

Exodus 34:14 (for you shall worship no other god, for the Lord, whose name is Jealous, is a jealous God),

Psalm 47:7 For God is the King of all the earth; sing praises with a psalm!

Psalm 7:17 I will give to the Lord the thanks due to his righteousness, and I will sing praise to the name of the Lord, the Most High.

3

WHO IS JESUS?

As complex as God is, understanding who Jesus is may be even be more difficult.

Let's start with His life. He was born a Jew in Bethlehem, a small city in Israel, around 3 BC, during a time when the Romans ruled most of Europe and the surrounding regions. His parents were Joseph and Mary, and they lived in Nazareth, where Jesus grew up and worked. Matt. 2:1 / Luke 2:16 / Matt. 2:23

His parents were devoted Jews, and tried to honor God with their lives. After Jesus was twelve, we don't hear of Joseph again. But we know Jesus, around adulthood, earned a living as a carpenter, the trade His father taught Him. Mark 6:3 / Matt. 13:55

The first time we read about Jesus as an adult is when John the Baptist baptizes Him at age thirty. This begins His ministry. Matt. 3:13

He soon recruited twelve men—apostles—to follow Him in His ministry. Matt. 10:2

Jesus spent the next three years preaching God's message, until He was arrested by the Jewish leaders for presenting Himself as having the authority of God. These Jewish leaders worked it out with the Romans so the Romans would sentence Him to death. The same day the Romans sentenced Him, they crucified Him. Matt. 27:12 / Matt. 9:3 / Matt. 27:22

The Messiah

As you read that short summary of His life, you may have thought of many other things Jesus is known for.

Let's back up a little bit, and look at the Old Testament. It says at some point in the future, the Messiah, God's servant:

Isa. 9:1-2	• Will be a great light
Isa. 10:27	• Will break the burden on the people
1 Chron. 17:12	• His government (and throne) will reign forever
Ps. 22:28	• All the nations will serve Him
Isa. 9:7	• His peace will never cease to grow
Dan. 9:24	• He will be the Righteous Branch of David (meaning He will be without sin, and of the lineage of David)
Zeph. 3:19	• He will turn the people's shame into praise

Throughout history, since the time of Moses, the Jewish people talked about and read about this coming Messiah. He was their great hope. In general, they expected Him to come in as a conquering king, to deliver the people from the oppressive governments that ruled them. They didn't understand He would be God, coming to deliver them from their own oppressive sins, and that He would be the Messiah for all mankind, not just the Jewish nation.

Ps. 12:5
Ps. 72:4
1 Sam. 2:10

Birth and Early Life

At the birth of Jesus, it became obvious there was something special about Him:

Luke 1:26-27	• Mary was visited by an angel, who told her she would become pregnant, and that it was from God. They also said who the child would be—the coming King whose throne would last forever.
Luke 1:30-33	
Luke 1:34	• Mary became pregnant as a virgin—a miracle of God.
Matt. 1:20-21	• Joseph was visited by an angel in a dream, and he was told about Mary's pregnancy, that it was from God, and their son would save the people from their sins.
Matt. 1:24	
Luke 2:34,38	• Shepherds, on the day Jesus was born, were told the Messiah ("Christ" in Greek) was born, and where to find Him. They went to visit Him.
	• Simeon and Anna, elderly prophets, when they

11

saw Jesus, told His parents Jesus would be the salvation of the people. | Luke 2:8-9,15-16

- A star appeared in the sky that showed wise men from the east the King of the Jews had been born. They traveled to see Jesus (possibly months or years after His birth), visiting Jesus when He lived in a house, and they brought three gifts with them—gold, frankincense, and myrrh. They also paused to worship Him. | Matt. 2:1-2 Matt. 2:10-11

We know little about Jesus' life before His ministry. We know after Joseph and Mary had Jesus, they had other children. Jesus was their oldest child, but His siblings were step-siblings, because Joseph was not the biological father of Jesus. | Matt. 12:46 Matt. 13:55

We do know Jesus, even as a youth of twelve, showed wisdom in regards to spiritual things. When His parents found Him in the midst of the teachers of the temple, He was asking the teachers questions, showing great understanding, and even giving them answers. | Luke 2:41-42 Luke 2:46-47

Jesus' Ministry

When Jesus was thirty, He left His home in Nazareth to begin His ministry. This is when Jesus was baptized by John the Baptist, who was a prophet. | Matt. 3:13

After that, many events in Jesus' life are recorded in the Gospels, the first four books of the New Testament (Matthew, Mark, Luke, and John). Each gives a biography of Jesus' life. These show that for most of the time over the next three years, before His crucifixion, Jesus lived and traveled in the northern region of Israel called Galilee. His crucifixion was in Jerusalem, in the southern region of Israel. | Luke 1:1-4 Matt. 4:23 Mark 10:33

In planning for His future church, Jesus needed His message to be carried on after He gave His life on the cross, so He recruited twelve men to travel with Him, to train them in all the concepts of God that He wanted mankind to know and understand. They were called the twelve apostles, or sometimes called the twelve disciples, although a disciple is anyone who follows Jesus. The name apostle has a very specific meaning, referring to these | Luke 6:13

twelve men. Over the three years before His death, these men went everywhere with Him.

Jesus had three years to basically do two things—show He was truthful and legitimate, and teach about God and spiritual things. This disappointed some, who wanted the Christ to be their King That is what Judas wanted. Eventually he felt betrayed by Jesus turned against Him.

Jesus constantly taught the apostles and anyone who would listen. He often paused during the day to preach, the most famous of which is called the Sermon on the Mount (see Matthew 5-7). Many times He would tell stories called parables, to teach specific lessons.

In His teachings, He was always bold to tell the truth. He had the perfect perception of God, so He was able to discern the hearts of those He was talking with. If the heart was sour, He would tell them. And if the heart was right, He would praise them. He expected people to try to be good, and that their goal should be God's perfection.

But to prove His authority and godly position as the Son of God, He often performed miracles.

- At a wedding, when the wine ran out, He turned water into wine, even better than the wine that was first served.

- He fed thousands of people, multiplying small amounts of food into more than everyone needed.

- A good friend of His, Lazarus, had died. He was so touched He cried. After four days, He traveled to where Lazarus' body was, and brought him back to life.

- He fixed the eyes of blind people so they could see.

- He fixed the legs of lame people so they could walk.

- He had authority over demons, and forced them to leave people alone.

- He walked on water, and allowed Peter to do the same

John 14:6-7
John 6:15
Matt. 27:3
Mark 14:45
Matt. 7:28
Mark 1:14
Matt. 5:1-2
Matt. 13:3

John 12:49

Matt. 9:4

Matt. 5:48

John 2:9

Mat 14:20-21

John 11:14,43

Matt. 11:5

Matt. 8:32

Matt. 14:26

• He stopped a storm, so the weather became calm	Matt. 8:27
• He prevented angry mobs from harming Him, long before it was His time for the crucifixion.	Luke 4:29-30

Jesus' Character

Jesus was around a lot of people, a lot of the time. When people spent time with Him, they got to see His true nature, His character. And the strange thing… the character of Jesus was the same as what they knew God to be like.   **John 14:7**

Because of Jesus' love, He responds to those who follow Him. Those who make the effort to have a heart for God with Jesus as the Christ (the one who brings us to God), see that He is: **John 15:9**

• Gracious—He gave others what they didn't deserve or earn	John 8:11
• Merciful—He doesn't punish His followers in the way they *do* deserve	Luke 22:24,32
• Patient—He continuously hopes the best for us despite the many times we let Him down	
• Kind—He always treats us softly	Matt. 9:36
• Joyful—We don't often associate Jesus with this attribute, but Jesus' experiences are fun, rich, and full	John 15:11
• Faithful—Jesus never changes, and can always be trusted—He will be there for you	
• Peaceful—Jesus loves harmony, and He is so full of peace we almost can't imagine it	Matt. 28:20
• Good—Jesus is good, because He is like God	John 14:27
• Empathetic—As a human, He can relate to us	
• Controlled—He does nothing without thought and planning—it is always without regret	Heb. 12:15

Jesus is perfect. And as a result, Jesus also has high standards for us:

• He tells us we can only go to God through Him	Matt. 21:12-13
• He desires perfection from us	Matt. 5:48

Luke 14:26-27	• He wants our love for God to be greater than our love for any other person or thing

Jesus' Claims

Jesus made many statements that clearly set Him apart, that identified who He was, that showed His godliness and identity as the Christ:

John 3:16	• He said God had sent Him.
Matt. 11:10	• He said God had told of the coming of Jesus.
John 6:46	• Jesus said no one else had seen the Father, except for Him.
John 14:7	• Jesus said to know Him is to know the Father. If we've seen Him, we've seen the Father.
John 12:49	• Jesus said the words He speaks were given to Him by the Father.
Mark 2:5	• He claimed to have authority to forgive sins.
John 3:36	• He claimed to have authority over death and life.
John 5:20	• He said God shows Him all the things that God is doing in the world.
John 5:21	• He said He can give eternal life to whom He wishes.
John 5:23	• He claimed those who do not honor Him, are not honoring the Father.
Matt. 28:18	• Jesus claimed to have all authority in both heaven and earth, especially above any earthly rulers.
John 14:6	• He said the only way to know the Father is to also know Him.

Jesus' Position

Col. 1:16 John 1:1,14	Jesus existed before all creation. When God created the Universe and all that is in it, everything was created through Jesus. So Jesus, as part of God, helped create everything, including mankind. Understanding the high position Jesus had during creation shows how incredible it was for Him to become a man, and to sacrifice the way He did.

Because of the sacrifice Jesus did for us, He has placed

Himself in the position of being our conduit to God. It is how we get to have a relationship with God. Without Jesus' sacrifice, we would have no means to have a relationship with God. We'd need to be perfect to be able to be with God. He would require us to be completely free from sin to be in His presence. But we all have sinned. We have all done things in our life that go against what God requires us to do. Because we cannot be perfect, we are totally stuck. We are guilty—we have sinned. Unless someone intervenes for us, we are destined to live apart from God. But someone *did* intervene—Jesus the Christ, the Messiah. Just as anyone guilty in our court system has to pay the penalties of fines or imprisonment, we are guilty and must pay the penalties. But, Jesus paid the penalties for us, so through Him, as Christians, we are now considered free from sin in God's eyes. We still sin, but Jesus' one-time sacrifice continues to pay our penalties.

Phil. 2:7

Acts 4:12

Ps. 53:2-3

Rom. 3:5

Rom. 3:23

1 Cor. 7:23
Rom. 8:2
1 John 1:9

Jesus, as part of God, pre-existed everything, but became a human for us. This is an important concept to understand—Jesus' primary purpose on earth is to bring us to God, which we cannot do ourselves. When we talk to Jesus, we are to praise Him, honor Him, and thank Him for the greatest gift ever given, far beyond any other.

Gen. 1:26
1 Pet. 3:18

John 5:23
2 Cor. 9:15

Jesus paid for our sins with His life, His blood. God's requirement throughout history was the payment for sins is pure blood. In the Old Testament, each year, the Jews' payment to God for their sins was the blood of animals (although, this payment was weak and incomplete, and therefore temporary). But Jesus' giving of Himself was the final payment, once for all, for all mankind, for all sins, so that no more payment is required by God, who required blood from a pure giver. With animals, it had to be blood from an unblemished animal, without defects. With Jesus, because he had never sinned, His blood was pure.

1 Cor. 15:3

Lev. 1:3
Col. 2:17
Rom. 10:3-4

Heb. 9:12

Heb. 10:10
1 Pet. 1:19

Jesus's death was the central point of all of history, because this act is what allows us to have a relationship with God. All people before looked forward to, and all people afterwards looked back on, this moment in time.

2 Cor. 6:16
John 14:6

After Jesus' death, He was gone for three days. (It is not clear where Jesus actually went for those three days.) We say "three" days, because when the Jews counted a

Matt. 12:40
1 Cor. 15:4

day, it was any part of a day. He was gone for part of Friday, Saturday, and Sunday. He returned on the third day, and His body was restored to a healthy, functioning body, although the scars from the crucifixion remained on Him. Jesus' return to life is called the resurrection.

John 20:27
Acts 4:33

After Jesus' resurrection and going up to heaven ("ascension"), He now sits at the right hand of God, with all authority over heaven and earth underneath Him. Jesus talks to God for those who are Christians, i.e., those who have belief and faith in Jesus to cover their sins. Jesus asks for things we need, God already knows, but Jesus is supporting us before God. Jesus is continually talking to God for our benefit.

Acts 1:9
Mark 16:19

Rom. 8:34
John 17:20

Jesus' resurrection validated His godliness. It proclaimed to the world that everything He had done and taught was true and legitimate. It showed His power over death, and by implication, over both the physical and the spiritual death (i.e., separation from God when you die). People of faith in Jesus, after death, will not be separated from God, but will be joined to Him. They have spiritual life. Jesus died and came alive again, and by faith in Him, we also come alive, having spiritual life.

Eph. 2:13
1 Pet. 3:18

John 3:5

Jesus, for the next forty days, spent time with the apostles and hundreds of His disciples. At the end of the forty days, God lifted Jesus into the clouds and He vanished physically from them (He "ascended into heaven"). Just before leaving earth, He told His disciples He would be with them, even to the end of the world. As then, He now is with each believer. Because of Jesus, God also is with every believer. And, we'll see that every believer has the Holy Spirit with them.

Acts 1:3
Acts 1:9

Matt. 28:20

1 Cor. 3:16

Because Jesus is present everywhere, He is both with God in heaven and with each believer. He sees what our needs are, and is actively praying for us.

Rom. 8:34
Heb. 7:24-25

Picture Jesus holding our hand, bringing us to God. He stands by our side as we talk to God, love God, receive God's blessings. How do we talk to God? See the Lord's Prayer as an example. We praise God, ask for things, pray for others, thank Him, and in general, talk to God about everything in our life.

Matt. 6:9

In a way, this shows Jesus' great humility. His primary role with us is to get us to focus on God the Father. This is what His entire ministry was about—bringing us to God, and then teaching us to focus on God. May we praise and honor Jesus for what He has done for us.

Phil. 2:6
1 Pet. 3:18

Verses from this section:

Matthew 2:1 Now after Jesus was born in Bethlehem of Judea in the days of Herod the king, behold, wise men from the east came to Jerusalem,

Luke 2:16 And they went with haste and found Mary and Joseph, and the baby lying in a manger.

Matthew 2:23 And he went and lived in a city called Nazareth, so that what was spoken by the prophets might be fulfilled, that he would be called a Nazarene.

Mark 6:3 Is not this the carpenter, the son of Mary and brother of James and Joses and Judas and Simon? And are not his sisters here with us?" And they took offense at him.

Matthew 13:55 Is not this the carpenter's son? Is not his mother called Mary? And are not his brothers James and Joseph and Simon and Judas?

Matthew 3:13 Then Jesus came from Galilee to the Jordan to John, to be baptized by him.

Matthew 10:2 The names of the twelve apostles are these: first, Simon, who is called Peter, and Andrew his brother; James the son of Zebedee, and John his brother;

Matthew 27:12 But when he was accused by the chief priests and elders, he gave no answer.

Matthew 9:3 And behold, some of the scribes said to themselves, "This man is blaspheming."

Matthew 27:22 Pilate said to them, "Then what shall I do with Jesus who is called Christ?" They all said, "Let him be crucified!"

Isaiah 9:1-2 But there will be no gloom for her who was in anguish. In the former time he brought into contempt the land of Zebulun and the land of Naphtali, but in the latter time he has made glorious the way of the sea, the land beyond the Jordan, Galilee of the nations. The people who walked in darkness have seen a great light; those who dwelt in a land of deep darkness, on them has light shone.

Isaiah 10:27 And in that day his burden will depart from your shoulder, and his yoke from your neck; and the yoke will be broken because of the fat."

1 Chronicles 17:12 He shall build a house for me, and I will establish his throne forever.

Psalm 22:28 For kingship belongs to the Lord, and he rules over the nations.

Isaiah 9:7 Of the increase of his government and of peace there will be no end, on the throne of David and over his kingdom, to establish it and to uphold it with justice and with righteousness from this time forth and forevermore. The zeal of the Lord of hosts will do this.

Daniel 9:24 "Seventy weeks are decreed about your people and your holy city, to finish the transgression, to put an end to sin, and to atone for iniquity, to bring in everlasting righteousness, to seal both vision and prophet, and to anoint a most holy place.

Zephaniah 3:19 Behold, at that time I will deal with all your oppressors. And I will save the lame and gather the outcast, and I will change their shame into praise and renown in all the earth.

Psalm 12:5 "Because the poor are plundered, because the needy groan, I will now arise," says the Lord; "I will place him in the safety for which he longs."

Psalm 72:4 May he defend the cause of the poor of the people, give deliverance to the children of the needy, and crush the oppressor!

1 Samuel 2:10 The adversaries of the Lord shall be broken to pieces; against them he will thunder in heaven. The Lord will judge the ends of the earth; he will give strength to his king and exalt the horn of his anointed."

Luke 1:26-27 In the sixth month the angel Gabriel was sent from God to a city of Galilee named Nazareth, to a virgin betrothed to a man whose name was Joseph, of the house of David. And the virgin's name was Mary.

Luke 1:30 And the angel said to her, "Do not be afraid, Mary, for you have found favor with God.

Luke 1:31 And behold, you will conceive in your womb and bear a son, and you shall call his name Jesus.

Luke 1:32 He will be great and will be called the Son of the Most High. And the Lord God will give to him the throne of his father David,

Luke 1:33 and he will reign over the house of Jacob forever, and of his kingdom there will be no end."

Luke 1:34 And Mary said to the angel, "How will this be, since I am a virgin?"

Matthew 1:20-21 But as he considered these things, behold, an angel of the Lord appeared to him in a dream, saying, "Joseph, son of David, do not fear to take Mary as your wife, for that which is conceived in her is from the Holy Spirit. She will bear a son, and you shall call his name Jesus, for he will save his people from their sins."

Matthew 1:24 When Joseph woke from sleep, he did as the angel of the Lord commanded him: he took his wife,

Luke 2:8-9 And in the same region there were shepherds out in the field, keeping watch over their flock by night. And an angel of the Lord appeared to them, and the glory of the Lord shone around them, and they were filled with great fear.

Luke 2:15-16 When the angels went away from them into heaven, the shepherds said to one another, "Let us go over to Bethlehem and see this thing that has happened, which the Lord has made known to us." And they went with haste and found Mary and Joseph, and the baby lying in a manger.

Luke 2:34 And Simeon blessed them and said to Mary his mother, "Behold, this child is appointed for the fall and rising of many in Israel, and for a sign that is opposed

Luke 2:38 And coming up at that very hour she began to give thanks to God and to speak of him to all who were waiting for the redemption of Jerusalem.

Matthew 2:1-2 Now after Jesus was born in Bethlehem of Judea in the days of Herod the king, behold, wise men from the east came to Jerusalem, saying, "Where is he who has been born king of the Jews? For we saw his star when it rose and have come to worship him."

Matthew 2:10-11 When they saw the star, they rejoiced exceedingly with great joy. And going into the house they saw the child with Mary his mother, and they fell down and worshiped him. Then, opening their treasures, they offered him gifts, gold and frankincense and myrrh.

Matthew 12:46 While he was still speaking to the people, behold, his mother and his brothers stood outside, asking to speak to him.

Matthew 13:55 Is not this the carpenter's son? Is not his mother called Mary? And are not his brothers James and Joseph and Simon and Judas?

Luke 2:41-42 Now his parents went to Jerusalem every year at the Feast of the Passover. And when he was twelve years old, they went up according to custom.

Luke 2:46-47 After three days they found him in the temple, sitting among the teachers, listening to them and asking them questions. And all who heard him were amazed at his understanding and his answers.

Matthew 3:13 Then Jesus came from Galilee to the Jordan to John, to be baptized by him.

Luke 1:1 Inasmuch as many have undertaken to compile a narrative of the things that have been accomplished among us,

Luke 1:2 just as those who from the beginning were eyewitnesses and ministers of the word have delivered them to us,

Luke 1:3 it seemed good to me also, having followed all things closely for some time past, to write an orderly account for you, most excellent Theophilus,

Luke 1:4 that you may have certainty concerning the things you have been taught.

Matthew 4:23 And he went throughout all Galilee, teaching in their synagogues and proclaiming the gospel of the kingdom and healing every disease and every affliction among the people.

Mark 10:33 saying, "See, we are going up to Jerusalem, and the Son of Man will be delivered over to the chief priests and the scribes, and they will condemn him to death and deliver him over to the Gentiles.

Luke 6:13 And when day came, he called his disciples and chose from them twelve, whom he named apostles:

John 14:6 Jesus said to him, "I am the way, and the truth, and the life. No one comes to the Father except through me.

John 14:7 If you had known me, you would have known my Father also. From now on you do know him and have seen him."

John 6:15 Perceiving then that they were about to come and take him by force to make him king, Jesus withdrew again to the mountain by himself.

Matthew 27:3 Then when Judas, his betrayer, saw that Jesus was condemned, he changed his mind and brought back the thirty pieces of silver to the chief priests and the elders,

Mark 14:45 And when he came, he went up to him at once and said, "Rabbi!" And he kissed him.

Matthew 7:28 And when Jesus finished these sayings, the crowds were astonished at his teaching,

Mark 1:14 Now after John was arrested, Jesus came into Galilee, proclaiming the gospel of God,

Matthew 5:1-2 Seeing the crowds, he went up on the mountain, and when he sat down, his disciples came to him. And he opened his mouth and taught them, saying:

Matthew 13:3 And he told them many things in parables, saying: "A sower went out to sow.

John 12:49 For I have not spoken on my own authority, but the Father who sent me has himself given me a commandment—what to say and what to speak.

Matthew 9:4 But Jesus, knowing their thoughts, said, "Why do you think evil in your hearts?

Matthew 5:48 You therefore must be perfect, as your heavenly Father is perfect.

John 2:9 When the master of the feast tasted the water now become wine, and did not know where it came from (though the servants who had drawn the water knew), the master of the feast called the bridegroom

Matthew 14:20-21 And they all ate and were satisfied. And they took up twelve baskets full of the broken pieces left over. And those who ate were about five thousand men, besides women and children.

John 11:14 Then Jesus told them plainly, "Lazarus has died,

John 11:43 When he had said these things, he cried out with a loud voice, "Lazarus, come out."

Matthew 11:5 the blind receive their sight and the lame walk, lepers are cleansed and the deaf hear, and the dead are raised up, and the poor have good news preached to them.

Matthew 8:32 And he said to them, "Go." So they came out and went into the pigs, and behold, the whole herd rushed down the steep bank into the sea and drowned in the waters.

Matthew 14:26 But when the disciples saw him walking on the sea, they were terrified, and said, "It is a ghost!" and they cried out in fear.

Matthew 8:27 And the men marveled, saying, "What sort of man is this, that even winds and sea obey him?"

Luke 4:29-30 And they rose up and drove him out of the town and brought him to the brow of the hill on which their town was built, so that they could throw him down the cliff. But passing through their midst, he went away.

John 14:7 If you had known me, you would have known my Father also. From now on you do know him and have seen him."

John 15:9 As the Father has loved me, so have I loved you. Abide in my love.

John 8:11 She said, "No one, Lord." And Jesus said, "Neither do I condemn you; go, and from now on sin no more."

Luke 22:24 A dispute also arose among them, as to which of them was to be regarded as the greatest.

Luke 22:32 but I have prayed for you that your faith may not fail. And when you have turned again, strengthen your brothers."

Matthew 9:36 When he saw the crowds, he had compassion for them, because they were harassed and helpless, like sheep without a shepherd.

John 15:11 These things I have spoken to you, that my joy may be in you, and that your joy may be full.

Matthew 28:20 teaching them to observe all that I have commanded you. And behold, I am with you always, to the end of the age."

John 14:27 Peace I leave with you; my peace I give to you. Not as the world gives do I give to you. Let not your hearts be troubled, neither let them be afraid.

Hebrews 12:15 See to it that no one fails to obtain the grace of God; that no "root of bitterness" springs up and causes trouble, and by it many become defiled;

Matthew 21:12-13 And Jesus entered the temple and drove out all who sold and bought in the temple, and he overturned the tables of the money-changers and the seats of those who sold pigeons. He said to them, "It is written, 'My house shall be called a house of prayer,' but you make it a den of robbers."

Matthew 5:48 You therefore must be perfect, as your heavenly Father is perfect.

Luke 14:26-27 "If anyone comes to me and does not hate his own father and mother and wife and children and brothers and sisters, yes, and even his own life, he cannot be my disciple. Whoever does not bear his own cross and come after me cannot be my disciple.

John 3:16 "For God so loved the world, that he gave his only Son, that whoever believes in him should not perish but have eternal life.

Matthew 11:10 This is he of whom it is written, "'Behold, I send my messenger before your face, who will prepare your way before you.'

John 6:46 not that anyone has seen the Father except he who is from God; he has seen the Father.

John 14:7 If you had known me, you would have known my Father also. From now on you do know him and have seen him."

John 12:49 For I have not spoken on my own authority, but the Father who sent me has himself given me a commandment—what to say and what to speak.

Mark 2:5 And when Jesus saw their faith, he said to the paralytic, "Son, your sins are forgiven."

John 3:36 Whoever believes in the Son has eternal life; whoever does not obey the Son shall not see life, but the wrath of God remains on him.

John 5:20 For the Father loves the Son and shows him all that he himself is doing. And greater works than these will he show him, so that you may marvel.

John 5:21 For as the Father raises the dead and gives them life, so also the Son gives life to whom he will.

John 5:23 that all may honor the Son, just as they honor the Father. Whoever does not honor the Son does not honor the Father who sent him.

Matthew 28:18 And Jesus came and said to them, "All authority in heaven and on earth has been given to me.

John 14:6 Jesus said to him, "I am the way, and the truth, and the life. No one comes to the Father except through me.

Colossians 1:16 For by him all things were created, in heaven and on earth, visible and invisible, whether thrones or dominions or rulers or authorities—all things were created through him and for him.

John 1:1 In the beginning was the Word, and the Word was with God, and the Word was God.

John 1:14 And the Word became flesh and dwelt among us, and we have seen his glory, glory as of the only Son from the Father, full of grace and truth.

Philippians 2:7 but emptied himself, by taking the form of a servant, being born in the likeness of men.

Acts 4:12 And there is salvation in no one else, for there is no other name under heaven given among men by which we must be saved."

Psalm 53:2-3 God looks down from heaven on the children of man to see if there are any who understand, who seek after God. They have all fallen away; together they have become corrupt; there is none who does good, not even one.

Romans 3:5 But if our unrighteousness serves to show the righteousness of God, what shall we say? That God is unrighteous to inflict wrath on us? (I speak in a human way.)

Romans 3:23 for all have sinned and fall short of the glory of God,

1 Corinthians 7:23 You were bought with a price; do not become bondservants of men.

Romans 8:2 For the law of the Spirit of life has set you free in Christ Jesus from the law of sin and death.

1 John 1:9 If we confess our sins, he is faithful and just to forgive us our sins and to cleanse us from all unrighteousness.

Genesis 1:26 Then God said, "Let us make man in our image, after our likeness. And let them have dominion over the fish of the sea and over the birds of the heavens and over the livestock and over all the earth and over every creeping thing that creeps on the earth."

1 Peter 3:18 For Christ also suffered once for sins, the righteous for the unrighteous, that he might bring us to God, being put to death in the flesh but made alive in the spirit,

John 5:23 that all may honor the Son, just as they honor the Father. Whoever does not honor the Son does not honor the Father who sent him.

2 Corinthians 9:15 Thanks be to God for his inexpressible gift!

1 Corinthians 15:3 For I delivered to you as of first importance what I also received: that Christ died for our sins in accordance with the Scriptures,

Leviticus 1:3 "If his offering is a burnt offering from the herd, he shall offer a male without blemish. He shall bring it to the entrance of the tent of meeting, that he may be accepted before the Lord.

Colossians 2:17 These are a shadow of the things to come, but the substance belongs to Christ.

Romans 10:3-4 For, being ignorant of the righteousness of God, and seeking to establish their own, they did not submit to God's righteousness. For Christ is the end of the law for righteousness to everyone who believes.

Hebrews 9:12 he entered once for all into the holy places, not by means of the blood of goats and calves but by means of his own blood, thus securing an eternal redemption.

Hebrews 10:10 And by that will we have been sanctified through the offering of the body of Jesus Christ once for all.

1 Peter 1:19 but with the precious blood of Christ, like that of a lamb without blemish or spot.

2 Corinthians 6:16 What agreement has the temple of God with idols? For we are the temple of the living God; as God said, "I will make my dwelling among them and walk among them, and I will be their God, and they shall be my people.

John 14:6 Jesus said to him, "I am the way, and the truth, and the life. No one comes to the Father except through me.

Matthew 12:40 For just as Jonah was three days and three nights in the belly of the great fish, so will the Son of Man be three days and three nights in the heart of the earth.

1 Corinthians 15:4 that he was buried, that he was raised on the third day in accordance with the Scriptures,

John 20:27 Then he said to Thomas, "Put your finger here, and see my hands; and put out your hand, and place it in my side. Do not disbelieve, but believe."

Acts 4:33 And with great power the apostles were giving their testimony to the resurrection of the Lord Jesus, and great grace was upon them all.

Acts 1:9 And when he had said these things, as they were looking on, he was lifted up, and a cloud took him out of their sight.

Mark 16:19 So then the Lord Jesus, after he had spoken to them, was taken up into heaven and sat down at the right hand of God.

Romans 8:34 Who is to condemn? Christ Jesus is the one who died—more than that, who was raised— who is at the right hand of God, who indeed is interceding for us.

John 17:20 "I do not ask for these only, but also for those who will believe in me through their word,

Ephesians 2:13 But now in Christ Jesus you who once were far off have been brought near by the blood of Christ.

1 Peter 3:18 For Christ also suffered once for sins, the righteous for the unrighteous, that he might bring us to God, being put to death in the flesh but made alive in the spirit,

John 3:5 Jesus answered, "Truly, truly, I say to you, unless one is born of water and the Spirit, he cannot enter the kingdom of God.

Acts 1:3 He presented himself alive to them after his suffering by many proofs, appearing to them during forty days and speaking about the kingdom of God.

Acts 1:9 And when he had said these things, as they were looking on, he was lifted up, and a cloud took him out of their sight.

Matthew 28:20 teaching them to observe all that I have commanded you. And behold, I am with you always, to the end of the age."

1 Corinthians 3:16 Do you not know that you are God's temple and that God's Spirit dwells in you?

Romans 8:34 Who is to condemn? Christ Jesus is the one who died—more than that, who was raised— who is at the right hand of God, who indeed is interceding for us.

Hebrews 7:24-25 but he holds his priesthood permanently, because he continues forever. Consequently, he is able to save to the uttermost those who draw near to God through him, since he always lives to make intercession for them.

Matthew 6:9 Pray then like this: "Our Father in heaven, hallowed be your name.

Philippians 2:6 who, though he was in the form of God, did not count equality with God a thing to be grasped,

1 Peter 3:18 For Christ also suffered once for sins, the righteous for the unrighteous, that he might bring us to God, being put to death in the flesh but made alive in the spirit,

4

WHO IS THE HOLY SPIRIT?

Most people have a pretty good understanding of who God the Father is and who Jesus is, but barely know who the Holy Spirit is. Yet all three are equal persons in God. What a perfect name for Him. It perfectly depicts who He is. He is holy, and He is a spirit.

Lev. 19:2

Holy—this is the exact character of God. "Holy" is defined as having the nature of God. The Holy Spirit has the exact nature of God. He is part of God, along with the Father and the Son. This is the Trinity. The holiness of the Holy Spirit shows He is God, an equal and proper part of the Trinity.

Exod. 31:3
Num. 27:18
Judg. 3:10

But as a spirit, what does He do? The Holy Spirit was very active with the Jewish people before Jesus. The Bible often tells of instances where the Holy Spirit was with different individuals. He dwelt with them and influenced them.

Acts 2:1-4

About a week after Jesus left earth physically (when He ascended), there was a Jewish festival called Pentecost. Jews from many regions and countries were in Jerusalem for that festival. During that particular festival, a very significant event took place that forever changed the life of believers. The apostles were all visiting together in a house, and they heard "noise like a violent rushing wind" that filled the house. They saw tongues of fire descend on each person. This was an indication the Holy Spirit was now *in* the believers, as compared to previously how the Holy Spirit would dwell *with* them. That day the apostles preached to thousands. The Holy Spirit gave them the ability to speak in the individual languages of those

Acts 2:6
Acts 2:41

present, so the listeners heard the gospel in their own tongue. Thousands became Christians, and received the gift of the Holy Spirit. From that point onward, the Holy

Rom. 8:9

Spirit no longer dwelt with believers, but in believers.

When we become a Christian, and the Holy Spirit comes in us, He seals us in our salvation through Christ. This is the guarantee of our relationship with God and of our destiny in heaven.

Eph. 1:13
Rom. 8:14

We have a relationship with God because of the sacrifice of Jesus and our faith in Him. God lives with and works with each Christian, taking care of events and circumstances, responding to prayers, etc. We have a personal and intimate relationship with Him. The Holy Spirit is also active in each Christian's life, but silently helping us take care of business.

Rom. 8:16

John 15:26

Jesus calls the Holy Spirit "the Helper." Let's look at how the Spirit works for us:

- He shows us what sin is. When we are tempted, He is actively telling our spirit not to go forward, and makes us very aware when we do sin. God's goal is for us to be like Him, and the Spirit works diligently toward that end.

  Rom. 8:4
  Rom. 14:17

- The Spirit is active in the process that makes it so our sins no longer cause us spiritual death, but we are regenerated into a new life. He renews us. This is a purpose for baptism—it is a demonstration of the cleansing we received from the Holy Spirit.

  1 Cor. 6:11
  Acts 2:38
  Rom. 8:11

- The Spirit is the great teacher, giving us wisdom and insight into all things pertaining to God. He teaches us what is truth and what is false. Because He is holy, what He teaches us is perfect truth, which means it will never conflict with Scripture.

  1 Cor. 2:12
  John 15:26

- He matures us in our walk with God. He helps us become who God wants us to be.

  Rom. 8:14

- The Spirit gives us power to do things that otherwise we would not be able to do. This might mean speaking about God, going boldly into difficult situations, fighting against temptation, etc.

  1 Cor. 2:4
  Rom. 15:19

- He gives us the words to say, particularly of the things of God, but also words that heal, when we

  1 Cor. 2:13

otherwise would have trouble speaking.

Rom. 8:26-27
- The Spirit prays for us, knowing what our deepest and critical needs are, way more than we even know ourselves. He works with the Father in every step of our lives.

1 Cor. 12:4

1 Cor. 12:7

In addition to all this, each believer receives special gifts from the Spirit, or "gifts of the Spirit." These are special abilities placed in believers at the time they receive the Holy Spirit. The Spirit can also choose to give more gifts later, as we continue to live and mature with God. The critical thing about these gifts is they are given by the Spirit to benefit others. Although, as a side benefit, we are also blessed. These abilities could be things like a supernatural ability to preach, to serve, to give, to teach, to heal, to perform miracles, or a supernatural knowledge, or wisdom, or speech (tongue). The Spirit gives one or more gifts to each believer, and works with the believer to use these gifts for the common good.

1 Cor. 12:8-10
Rom. 12:6-8

Each believer should work to understand which gifts God has given you, by studying the gifts and examining how God has been working in your life. Often you can detect what your gifts are by looking at what passions you have to help others. The Holy Spirit has placed these passions in your spirit to use your gifts.

Ps. 139:13
Matt. 25:15
Gen. 1:26
2 Cor. 3:17
Phil. 3:3
1 Tim. 3:16

Gifts of the Spirit need to be distinguished from the talents God has given you. When God created you, He gave you special talents. Talents you had before you became a Christian, but gifts you received afterwards. Every person has talents from God, but only believers have gifts of the Spirit. Talents are often used in vocational areas, but gifts are always used for the common good for spiritual benefits.

Heb. 10:15
2 Cor. 6:6

The Holy Spirit is the one who enables the proper use of gifts. It is important you allow the Holy Spirit to work in your life, and that your focus in using gifts is through Him, for others.

1 Cor. 6:19

Like God and Jesus, you have a relationship with the Holy Spirit, so you need to get to know Him. He has been around eternally with the Father and Son. He is all knowing, all-present, and all-loving, in the same way the Father and Son are.

As the Bible was being written, the Spirit guided the authors to write what God wanted written. God had a word to give to us. The Spirit made sure what God wanted written was written.

2 Sam. 23:2
2 Pet. 1:20-21

Because of the Spirit, we have the Bible. Because of the Spirit, we have the potential to live a great life with God. Carefully listen to what the Spirit tells and teaches your spirit. We often suppress His voice to us, but be open to giving Him free reign in your spirit.

John 14:26

Let's take a look at one of the most difficult concepts in all of theology—the concept of the Trinity. It is clear in Scripture each of these three are distinct persons, and have distinct roles. Yet, all are God, or maybe we can say part of God. The Bible does refer to Jesus as God in several places, so we can say that Jesus is God, but He is not God the Father. The unity between Jesus and God the Father is so close it is practically indistinguishable, so you could refer to Jesus as God the Father, but in general Jesus is referred to as the Son of God.

Heb. 1:8
John 10:30
John 14:9
Matt. 28:19
1 Cor. 3:16

God, the person, is the Father. That is God's position. Jesus is the Son. Those who have a relationship with God through Christ also are called sons and daughters of God, but Jesus' position is unique, special—He is "the" Son of God.

Mark 1:1

One of the most significant traits of the three in the Trinity that makes them unique, is they are omnipresent, meaning everywhere. They are the only persons, or beings, that are capable of this. This is one of the most outstanding things that distinguishes who God is. God, Jesus, and the Holy Spirit are involved in activities in the life of each and every person. The angels cannot do this— this includes the angels with God, and the fallen angels, like Satan. At any point in time, angels can only be in one place. Those who claim "the devil made me do it" most likely did not encounter the devil, but were influenced by some from his army of demons. Like us, the devil can only focus on one thing at a time.

Ezek. 36:27
2 Cor. 3:17

Philem. 1:5

2 Pet. 2:4
Rev. 12:9
1 Pet. 5:8

The Bible uses the term "saints" to refer to all Christians—that is, according to the Bible, every

Acts 9:13
Acts 9:32

Luke 16:22-23

Christian is a saint. Saints (Christians) who have died and are with God also cannot focus on more than one thing at a time. This is why there is no value in talking to saints who have long been dead. Even in the afterlife they can only be in one place at a time, so they cannot listen to each person.

We are not on our own. We have a relationship with God and we have peace with God, because Jesus enabled that. And we have the Holy Spirit, working in us in quiet and unseen ways, to bring us to where God wants us to go, and to be what God wants us to be.

Verses from this section:

Leviticus 19:2 "Speak to all the congregation of the people of Israel and say to them, You shall be holy, for I the Lord your God am holy.

Exodus 31:3 and I have filled him with the Spirit of God, with ability and intelligence, with knowledge and all craftsmanship,

Numbers 27:18 So the Lord said to Moses, "Take Joshua the son of Nun, a man in whom is the Spirit, and lay your hand on him.

Judges 3:10 The Spirit of the Lord was upon him, and he judged Israel. He went out to war, and the Lord gave Cushan-rishathaim king of Mesopotamia into his hand. And his hand prevailed over Cushan-rishathaim.

Acts 2:1 When the day of Pentecost arrived, they were all together in one place.

Acts 2:2 And suddenly there came from heaven a sound like a mighty rushing wind, and it filled the entire house where they were sitting.

Acts 2:3 And divided tongues as of fire appeared to them and rested on each one of them.

Acts 2:4 And they were all filled with the Holy Spirit and began to speak in other tongues as the Spirit gave them utterance.

Acts 2:6 And at this sound the multitude came together, and they were bewildered, because each one was hearing them speak in his own language.

Acts 2:41 So those who received his word were baptized, and there were added that day about three thousand souls.

Romans 8:9 You, however, are not in the flesh but in the Spirit, if in fact the Spirit of God dwells in you. Anyone who does not have the Spirit of Christ does not belong to him.

Ephesians 1:13 In him you also, when you heard the word of truth, the gospel of your salvation, and believed in him, were sealed with the promised Holy Spirit,

Romans 8:14 For all who are led by the Spirit of God are sons of God.

Romans 8:16 The Spirit himself bears witness with our spirit that we are children of God,

John 15:26 "But when the Helper comes, whom I will send to you from the Father, the Spirit of truth, who proceeds from the Father, he will bear witness about me.

Romans 8:4 in order that the righteous requirement of the law might be fulfilled in us, who walk not according to the flesh but according to the Spirit.

Romans 14:17 For the kingdom of God is not a matter of eating and drinking but of righteousness and peace and joy in the Holy Spirit.

1 Corinthians 6:11 And such were some of you. But you were washed, you were sanctified, you were justified in the name of the Lord Jesus Christ and by the Spirit of our God.

Acts 2:38 And Peter said to them, "Repent and be baptized every one of you in the name of Jesus Christ for the forgiveness of your sins, and you will receive the gift of the Holy Spirit.

Romans 8:11 If the Spirit of him who raised Jesus from the dead dwells in you, he who raised Christ Jesus from the dead will also give life to your mortal bodies through his Spirit who dwells in you.

1 Corinthians 2:12 Now we have received not the spirit of the world, but the Spirit who is from God, that we might understand the things freely given us by God.

John 15:26 "But when the Helper comes, whom I will send to you from the Father, the Spirit of truth, who proceeds from the Father, he will bear witness about me.

Romans 8:14 For all who are led by the Spirit of God are sons of God.

1 Corinthians 2:4 and my speech and my message were not in plausible words of wisdom, but in demonstration of the Spirit and of power,

Romans 15:19 by the power of signs and wonders, by the power of the Spirit of God—so that from Jerusalem and all the way around to Illyricum I have fulfilled the ministry of the gospel of Christ;

1 Corinthians 2:13 And we impart this in words not taught by human wisdom but taught by the Spirit, interpreting spiritual truths to those who are spiritual.

Romans 8:26-27 Likewise the Spirit helps us in our weakness. For we do not know what to pray for as we ought, but the Spirit himself intercedes for us with groanings too deep for words. And he who searches hearts knows what is the mind of the Spirit, because the Spirit intercedes for the saints according to the will of God.

1 Corinthians 12:4 Now there are varieties of gifts, but the same Spirit;

1 Corinthians 12:7 To each is given the manifestation of the Spirit for the common good.

1 Corinthians 12:8 For to one is given through the Spirit the utterance of wisdom, and to another the utterance of knowledge according to the same Spirit,

1 Corinthians 12:9 to another faith by the same Spirit, to another gifts of healing by the one Spirit,

1 Corinthians 12:10 to another the working of miracles, to another prophecy, to another the ability to distinguish between spirits, to another various kinds of tongues, to another the interpretation of tongues.

Romans 12:6 Having gifts that differ according to the grace given to us, let us use them: if prophecy, in proportion to our faith;

Romans 12:7 if service, in our serving; the one who teaches, in his teaching;

Romans 12:8 the one who exhorts, in his exhortation; the one who contributes, in generosity; the one who leads, with zeal; the one who does acts of mercy, with cheerfulness.

Psalm 139:13 For you formed my inward parts; you knitted me together in my mother's womb.

Matthew 25:15 To one he gave five talents, to another two, to another one, to each according to his ability. Then he went away.

Genesis 1:26 Then God said, "Let us make man in our image, after our likeness. And let them have dominion over the fish of the sea and over the birds of the heavens and over the livestock and over all the earth and over every creeping thing that creeps on the earth."

2 Corinthians 3:17 Now the Lord is the Spirit, and where the Spirit of the Lord is, there is freedom.

Philippians 3:3 For we are the circumcision, who worship by the Spirit of God and glory in Christ Jesus and put no confidence in the flesh—

1 Timothy 3:16 All Scripture is breathed out by God and profitable for teaching, for reproof, for correction, and for training in righteousness,

Hebrews 10:15 And the Holy Spirit also bears witness to us; for after saying,

2 Corinthians 6:6 by purity, knowledge, patience, kindness, the Holy Spirit, genuine love;

1 Corinthians 6:19 Or do you not know that your body is a temple of the Holy Spirit within you, whom you have from God? You are not your own,

2 Samuel 23:2 "The Spirit of the Lord speaks by me; his word is on my tongue."

2 Peter 1:20-21 knowing this first of all, that no prophecy of Scripture comes from someone's own interpretation. 21 For no prophecy was ever produced by the will of man, but men spoke from God as they were carried along by the Holy Spirit.

John 14:26 But the Helper, the Holy Spirit, whom the Father will send in my name, he will teach you all things and bring to your remembrance all that I have said to you.

Hebrews 1:8 But of the Son he says, "Your throne, O God, is forever and ever, the scepter of uprightness is the scepter of your kingdom.

John 10:30 I and the Father are one."

John 14:9 Jesus said to him, "Have I been with you so long, and you still do not know me, Philip? Whoever has seen me has seen the Father. How can you say, 'Show us the Father'?

Matthew 28:19 Go therefore and make disciples of all nations, baptizing them in the name of the Father and of the Son and of the Holy Spirit,

1 Corinthians 3:16 Do you not know that you are God's temple and that God's Spirit dwells in you?

Mark 1:1 The beginning of the gospel of Jesus Christ, the Son of God.

Ezekiel 36:27 And I will put my Spirit within you, and cause you to walk in my statutes and be careful to obey my rules.

2 Corinthians 3:17 Now the Lord is the Spirit, and where the Spirit of the Lord is, there is freedom.

Philemon 1:5 because I hear of your love and of the faith that you have toward the Lord Jesus and for all the saints,

2 Peter 2:4 For if God did not spare angels when they sinned, but cast them into hell and committed them to chains of gloomy darkness to be kept until the judgment;

Revelation 12:9 And the great dragon was thrown down, that ancient serpent, who is called the devil and Satan, the deceiver of the whole world— he was thrown down to the earth, and his angels were thrown down with him.

1 Peter 5:8 Be sober-minded; be watchful. Your adversary the devil prowls around like a roaring lion, seeking someone to devour.

Acts 9:13 But Ananias answered, "Lord, I have heard from many about this man, how much evil he has done to your saints at Jerusalem.

Acts 9:32 Now as Peter went here and there among them all, he came down also to the saints who lived at Lydda.

Luke 16:22-23 The poor man died and was carried by the angels to Abraham's side. The rich man also died and was buried, and in Hades, being in torment, he lifted up his eyes and saw Abraham far off and Lazarus at his side.

5

WHAT IS SIN?

When we talk of sin, we often think of the activities that are usually tied to that word—lying, stealing, cheating, etc. God does list sins like these in numerous passages in the Bible, most notably the Ten Commandments. But what other activities are considered sin?

> Exod. 20:3-17

Fundamentally, that is the wrong question. Instead of thinking of sins as a list of activities we should not be doing, let's understand what sin is at its core.

God is holy. Everything He does is pure and perfect. Holiness is a standard of how to think and act—like God. During Jesus' life on earth, He followed that standard. He was perfect. This standard is God's wish for us—"you are to be perfect, as your heavenly Father is perfect." Any time we don't follow that standard, whether knowingly or unknowingly, it is sin. Sin at its core is when we are thinking or doing anything that does not align with God's holiness, His character.

> Prov. 15:9
> Num. 32:13
> John 3:16
> Matt. 5:48
> Lev. 19:2
> Ps. 99:9
> 1 Pet. 2:21-22

This could be what we do, but also what we do not do. The Bible mentions when we "sin against the Lord by ceasing to pray" for a person when we should. There could be situations where we sin when we don't stand up for someone, when we don't have time for someone in need, when we ignore or allow evil, or when our silence implies a lie.

> Lev. 4:2
> Ps. 19:12
> 1 Sam. 12:23

God hates sin. He is repulsed when we sin, even angered. And for each sin, we are guilty before God. This is the beauty and incredulity of what God arranged through the death of Jesus. For every sin we commit, Jesus paid for it with His death. What a weight He has lifted off us! Through our faith in Jesus, Jesus paid the penalty of sin for us, and we are no longer guilty before God.

> Rom. 1:18
> Prov. 12:21
> Hab. 2:16
> 1 John 1:9
> Jude 1:24

Does this give us the freedom to do whatever we

Rom. 6:15
Rev. 3:16
Acts 8:21
Deut. 6:5
1 Kings 8:61

want? Paul in the Bible discusses this question, and concludes, "May it never be!" Sin still has consequences. It hurts people, it hurts ourselves, and it displeases God. Here is the key concept to know about our sin—God examines our heart. He looks for a heart for Him, and the effort to repent of sin and to do what He wants. He sees what is in our hearts, and what we are working toward, and this molds and defines our real relationship with Him.

Prov. 28:13

When people have a relationship with God, they often get too comfortable and don't pay attention to sin in their life. Sin that is not acknowledged or confronted can hinder your relationship with God. To confront sin, we need to have a good view of God's holiness, and what He wants for us. Let's look at some of the things God tells us are sin:

Phil. 4:11
1 Tim. 6:9
James 5:9
Phil. 2:3
Prov. 28:6
James 5:16
Ps. 1:2
Matt. 6:14

Eph. 5:18
Eccles. 7:9
James 1:19
Mark 9:35
Ps. 15:3
James 1:27
Rom. 1:28
Eph. 2:3
1 Thess. 4:3

Prov. 10:26
Eph. 4:13
James 3:16

- Not satisfied in life; jealous of others (looks, money, family, skills, position, etc.)
- Complaining (especially within the church)
- Wanting your own success above others
- Cheating on taxes or your time at work
- Doesn't admit faults; doesn't say sorry
- Lack of prayer or reading the Bible
- Cannot forgive…everyone
- Drunkenness
- Not patient
- Quick to anger
- Demanding your way, or that you are always right
- Talk about others negatively
- No servant heart to help others
- Inappropriate sexual thoughts or actions; what you look at or dwell on
- Wrong priorities or passions
- Laziness
- Bitterness
- Cause trouble because of selfishness

Obviously this is just scratching the surface.

Are we truly trying to follow God? Are we truly looking at ourselves in the mirror to see what's wrong? This is the heart God wants in us. Are we trying to follow Him, to do what is right, and making an effort toward that? God knows we will not be perfect. We absolutely cannot be. We will continue to sin. But God looks at our attitude toward sin—do we just ignore it, or are we making the effort to improve, mature, and overcome?

James 1:22-25

Rom. 3:23
Phil. 3:12

There are many things that are questionable. If you struggle with whether something is acceptable to God, maybe it would be better to simply avoid it, and avoid the struggle?

Don't make excuses. We may try to disguise sin as something good. We try to justify sin, and explain to God why we did something wrong. Check your spirit. See if the Holy Spirit is revealing to you whether something is sin.

John 14:26
1 Cor. 2:12-13

Maybe you have ignored the Spirit on so many occasions that it's hard to hear His voice now. You don't see your sin, and don't hear the Holy Spirit trying to catch your attention. Ask the Spirit to reveal to you your sin.

For others, it is the opposite—the weight of your sin is too heavy. You have suffered the consequences of poor decisions and have trouble in life because of it. Many who've given in to adultery have watched their family fall apart. Some who have abused drugs or alcohol for too long are dealing with their broken bodies. Gambling addictions have impoverished many. Others are in prison because of poor decisions. Go to God for forgiveness, and trust that God has forgiven you.

Ps. 38:4

Rom. 6:23
Gal. 3:10

Exod. 34:7

We do need to be aware sin has negative consequences. Many times it is obvious, but often we don't see these consequences. God makes is clear there will be negative results. The scariest thing about sin is it often can and will affect your family, and even generations afterwards. We should never think lightly of anything we do that disobeys God. Consequences to sin are similar with what happens when you throw an apple into the air. There is a result—it comes back down. The gravitational law requires it. The laws God has set in place regarding sin are similar—there is a consequence. But God can bring healing and restoration with honest repentance.

Gal. 6:7
Mal. 4:1

Hos. 6:1
Hos. 5:15
1 Cor. 15:57
Job 33:27

We usually have a warped view of our sin. We need to have the proper view—God's view. This is a tough challenge. In general, our view of our own sin is shaped by the consequences we have suffered with. If there have been few consequences, we tend to have a lighter view of our own sin. If the consequences have been very difficult, we carry our sin very heavily.

Let's look at how God views sin:

- God views anything not in line with His holiness as sin.
- God sees all sin. Nothing is hidden from His sight.
- God hates all sin. God does not ignore some sins.
- God hates all sin equally. He sees all sin as terrible, black, awful.
- Because of God's love for us, He works to guide us away from sin. He doesn't want us to sin.
- God accepts faith in Jesus as our full payment of sin. In Jesus, we are fully pardoned, forgiven. Jesus was the One punished for our sins.
- Through Jesus, our sins are removed far from us. God knows of our sin, but it is so distant, it practically does not exist, in God's eyes.
- Even with forgiveness, sin most likely will still have consequences. God may still punish for sin.
- God loves us completely, and is thrilled when He sees us loving Him and working on our sin. God will richly bless this faith and these efforts.

When you watch or read the news, you will see people doing despicable things. Certain things you see really get under your skin, really irritate or repulse you, like when children or women are harmed, or when innocent people are taken advantage of. You hate these actions. Yet, that is how God wants us to view all our sin. We need to see sin as God sees it, and to hate our sin as God hates it.

What is the proper way we should view our own sin?

Lev. 20:7

Ps. 139:3

1 John 2:6
Prov. 15:9

Ezek. 18:20

1 Pet. 3:18
Rom. 8:38-39

Ps. 103:12

Rom. 1:18

2 Cor. 9:8

- We are to hate sin as God hates it, and see it as it really is. | Rom. 3:10-12

- We are to repent of it, which means to confess it to God, and turn away from it. | 1 John 1:9

- We need to understand we are sinners, and we will continue to sin. | Rom. 3:23

- We need to understand *all* our sin is forgiven by God through our faith in Jesus. | Gen. 15:6 Rom. 3:22

- Again, the most important thing God looks for in us is our heart. Are we truly trying to follow Him? God looks at our attitude toward our own sin. | Luke 10:27

- Our sin may have tangible consequences. Because we are forgiven does not mean God removes all consequences from our thoughts or actions. | Prov. 12:13

- All sin can have consequences, even the private or hidden sins, that we think we have gotten away with, or that no one knows about. | Prov. 28:13 Ps. 90:8

- Your sin will affect your family. You may think they are removed from it, but they are not. God makes it clear in the Bible sin affects not only your generation but generations after. | Exod. 34:7

- God has a passion for us to do the right thing, to mature, to be like Him. Toward that end, God deals with our sin at different levels, depending on what our real need is. Sometimes God has to deal with us more severely to get our attention. And, other times, a softer, subtler approach is needed. | 2 Pet. 3:9

- God works with us. It comes down to what is going on in our hearts. Are we hiding sin, or are we confessing sin and working to mature? God will work with us if we go to Him honestly and with a passion for improvement. | Phil. 2:13

- We are not where we should be, but if going in the right direction, not where we used to be. | Phil. 3:12

It is important that we have a proper understanding of sin. We need to see sin as God see it. When you spend time in prayer and reading the Bible, examining what God tells us about our sin and His holiness, the more our eyes are opened. And, the more we will be discerning of what holiness is.

Phil. 1:6

Be honest about your sin. Defeat sin in your life. Find ways to win. Avoid situations that draw you to sin—you know what they are. Find verses that deal with your sin, and study and memorize them. Pray honestly to God to help you get on track with Him. Don't make excuses.

May the Holy Spirit reveal to you what sin is, may He build in you a heart toward God and His holiness, and may you listen and work toward the maturing God so wants for you. God loves you, and will bless you.

1 Cor. 2:10
Col. 1:9-12

Verses from this section:

Exodus 20:3 "You shall have no other gods before me.

Exodus 20:4 "You shall not make for yourself a carved image, or any likeness of anything that is in heaven above, or that is in the earth beneath, or that is in the water under the earth.

Exodus 20:5 You shall not bow down to them or serve them, for I the Lord your God am a jealous God, visiting the iniquity of the fathers on the children to the third and the fourth generation of those who hate me,

Exodus 20:6 but showing steadfast love to thousands of those who love me and keep my commandments.

Exodus 20:7 "You shall not take the name of the Lord your God in vain, for the Lord will not hold him guiltless who takes his name in vain.

Exodus 20:8 "Remember the Sabbath day, to keep it holy.

Exodus 20:9 Six days you shall labor, and do all your work,

Exodus 20:10 but the seventh day is a Sabbath to the Lord your God. On it you shall not do any work, you, or your son, or your daughter, your male servant, or your female servant, or your livestock, or the sojourner who is within your gates.

Exodus 20:11 For in six days the Lord made heaven and earth, the sea, and all that is in them, and rested on the seventh day. Therefore the Lord blessed the Sabbath day and made it holy.

Exodus 20:12 "Honor your father and your mother, that your days may be long in the land that the Lord your God is giving you.

Exodus 20:13 "You shall not murder.

Exodus 20:14 "You shall not commit adultery.

Exodus 20:15 "You shall not steal.

Exodus 20:16 "You shall not bear false witness against your neighbor.

Exodus 20:17 "You shall not covet your neighbor's house; you shall not covet your neighbor's wife, or his male servant, or his female servant, or his ox, or his donkey, or anything that is your neighbor's."

Proverbs 15:9 The way of the wicked is an abomination to the Lord, but he loves him who pursues righteousness.

Numbers 32:13 And the Lord 's anger was kindled against Israel, and he made them wander in the wilderness forty years, until all the generation that had done evil in the sight of the Lord was gone.

John 3:16 "For God so loved the world, that he gave his only Son, that whoever believes in him should not perish but have eternal life.

Matthew 5:48 You therefore must be perfect, as your heavenly Father is perfect.

Leviticus 19:2 Speak to all the congregation of the people of Israel and say to them, You shall be holy, for I the Lord your God am holy.

Psalm 99:9 Exalt the Lord our God, and worship at his holy mountain; for the Lord our God is holy!

1 Peter 2:21-22 For to this you have been called, because Christ also suffered for you, leaving you an example, so that you might follow in his steps. He committed no sin, neither was deceit found in his mouth.

Leviticus 4:2 "Speak to the people of Israel, saying, If anyone sins unintentionally in any of the Lord 's commandments about things not to be done, and does any one of them,

Psalm 19:12 Who can discern his errors? Declare me innocent from hidden faults.

1 Samuel 12:23 Moreover, as for me, far be it from me that I should sin against the Lord by ceasing to pray for you, and I will instruct you in the good and the right way.

Romans 1:18 For the wrath of God is revealed from heaven against all ungodliness and unrighteousness of men, who by their unrighteousness suppress the truth.

Proverbs 12:21 No ill befalls the righteous, but the wicked are filled with trouble.

Habakkuk 2:16 You will have your fill of shame instead of glory. Drink, yourself, and show your uncircumcision! The cup in the Lord 's right hand will come around to you, and utter shame will come upon your glory!

1 John 1:9 If we confess our sins, he is faithful and just to forgive us our sins and to cleanse us from all unrighteousness.

Jude 1:24 Now to him who is able to keep you from stumbling and to present you blameless before the presence of his glory with great joy,

Romans 6:15 What then? Are we to sin because we are not under law but under grace? By no means!

Revelation 3:16 So, because you are lukewarm, and neither hot nor cold, I will spit you out of my mouth.

Acts 8:21 You have neither part nor lot in this matter, for your heart is not right before God.

Deuteronomy 6:5 You shall love the Lord your God with all your heart and with all your soul and with all your might.

1 Kings 8:61 Let your heart therefore be wholly true to the Lord our God, walking in his statutes and keeping his commandments, as at this day."

Proverbs 28:13 Whoever conceals his transgressions will not prosper, but he who confesses and forsakes them will obtain mercy.

Philippians 4:11 Not that I am speaking of being in need, for I have learned in whatever situation I am to be content.

1 Timothy 6:9 But those who desire to be rich fall into temptation, into a snare, into many senseless and harmful desires that plunge people into ruin and destruction.

James 5:9 Do not grumble against one another, brothers, so that you may not be judged; behold, the Judge is standing at the door.

Philippians 2:3 Do nothing from selfish ambition or conceit, but in humility count others more significant than yourselves.

Proverbs 28:6 Better is a poor man who walks in his integrity than a rich man who is crooked in his ways.

James 5:16 Therefore, confess your sins to one another and pray for one another, that you may be healed. The prayer of a righteous person has great power as it is working.

Psalm 1:2 but his delight is in the law of the Lord, and on his law he meditates day and night.

Matthew 6:14 For if you forgive others their trespasses, your heavenly Father will also forgive you,

Ephesians 5:18 And do not get drunk with wine, for that is debauchery, but be filled with the Spirit,

Eccl 7:9 Be not quick in your spirit to become angry, for anger lodges in the heart of fools.

James 1:19 Know this, my beloved brothers: let every person be quick to hear, slow to speak, slow to anger;

Mark 9:35 And he sat down and called the twelve. And he said to them, "If anyone would be first, he must be last of all and servant of all."

Psalm 15:3 who does not slander with his tongue and does no evil to his neighbor, nor takes up a reproach against his friend;

James 1:27 Religion that is pure and undefiled before God, the Father, is this: to visit orphans and widows in their affliction, and to keep oneself unstained from the world.

Romans 1:28 And since they did not see fit to acknowledge God, God gave them up to a debased mind to do what ought not to be done.

Ephesians 2:3 among whom we all once lived in the passions of our flesh, carrying out the desires of the body and the mind, and were by nature children of wrath, like the rest of mankind.

1 Thessalonians 4:3 For this is the will of God, your sanctification: that you abstain from sexual immorality;

Proverbs 10:26 Like vinegar to the teeth and smoke to the eyes, so is the sluggard to those who send him.

Ephesians 4:13 until we all attain to the unity of the faith and of the knowledge of the Son of God, to mature manhood, to the measure of the stature of the fullness of Christ,

James 3:16 For where jealousy and selfish ambition exist, there will be disorder and every vile practice.

James 1:22 But be doers of the word, and not hearers only, deceiving yourselves.

James 1:23 For if anyone is a hearer of the word and not a doer, he is like a man who looks intently at his natural face in a mirror.

James 1:24 For he looks at himself and goes away and at once forgets what he was like.

James 1:25 But the one who looks into the perfect law, the law of liberty, and perseveres, being no hearer who forgets but a doer who acts, he will be blessed in his doing.

Romans 3:23 for all have sinned and fall short of the glory of God,

Philippians 3:12 Not that I have already obtained this or am already perfect, but I press on to make it my own, because Christ Jesus has made me his own.

John 14:26 But the Helper, the Holy Spirit, whom the Father will send in my name, he will teach you all things and bring to your remembrance all that I have said to you.

1 Corinthians 2:12-13 Now we have received not the spirit of the world, but the Spirit who is from God, that we might understand the things freely given us by God. And we impart this in words not taught by human wisdom but taught by the Spirit, interpreting spiritual truths to those who are spiritual.

Psalm 38:4 For my iniquities have gone over my head; like a heavy burden, they are too heavy for me.

Romans 6:23 For the wages of sin is death, but the free gift of God is eternal life in Christ Jesus our Lord.

Galatians 3:10 For all who rely on works of the law are under a curse; for it is written, "Cursed be everyone who does not abide by all things written in the Book of the Law, and do them."

Exodus 34:7 keeping steadfast love for thousands, forgiving iniquity and transgression and sin, but who will by no means clear the guilty, visiting the iniquity of the fathers on the children and the children's children, to the third and the fourth generation."

Galatians 6:7 Do not be deceived: God is not mocked, for whatever one sows, that will he also reap.

Malachi 4:1 For behold, the day is coming, burning like an oven, when all the arrogant and all evildoers will be stubble. The day that is coming shall set them ablaze, says the Lord of hosts, so that it will leave them neither root nor branch.

Hosea 6:1 "Come, let us return to the Lord; for he has torn us, that he may heal us; he has struck us down, and he will bind us up.

Hosea 5:15 I will return again to my place, until they acknowledge their guilt and seek my face, and in their distress earnestly seek me.

1 Corinthians 15:57 But thanks be to God, who gives us the victory through our Lord Jesus Christ.

Job 33:27 He sings before men and says: 'I sinned and perverted what was right, and it was not repaid to me.

Leviticus 20:7 Consecrate yourselves, therefore, and be holy, for I am the Lord your God.

Psalm 139:3 You search out my path and my lying down and are acquainted with all my ways.

1 John 2:6 whoever says he abides in him ought to walk in the same way in which he walked.

Proverbs 15:9 The way of the wicked is an abomination to the Lord, but he loves him who pursues righteousness.

Ezekiel 18:20 The soul who sins shall die. The son shall not suffer for the iniquity of the father, nor the father suffer for the iniquity of the son. The righteousness of the righteous shall be upon himself, and the wickedness of the wicked shall be upon himself.

1 Peter 3:18 For Christ also suffered once for sins, the righteous for the unrighteous, that he might bring us to God, being put to death in the flesh but made alive in the spirit,

Romans 8:38-39 For I am sure that neither death nor life, nor angels nor rulers, nor things present nor things to come, nor powers, nor height nor depth, nor anything else in all creation, will be able to separate us from the love of God in Christ Jesus our Lord.

Psalm 103:112 as far as the east is from the west, so far does he remove our transgressions from us.

Romans 1:18 For the wrath of God is revealed from heaven against all ungodliness and unrighteousness of men, who by their unrighteousness suppress the truth.

2 Corinthians 9:8 And God is able to make all grace abound to you, so that having all sufficiency in all things at all times, you may abound in every good work.

Romans 3:10-12 as it is written: "None is righteous, no, not one; no one understands; no one seeks for God. All have turned aside; together they have become worthless; no one does good, not even one."

1 John 1:9 If we confess our sins, he is faithful and just to forgive us our sins and to cleanse us from all unrighteousness.

Romans 3:23 for all have sinned and fall short of the glory of God,

Genesis 15:6 And he believed the Lord, and he counted it to him as righteousness.

Romans 3:22 the righteousness of God through faith in Jesus Christ for all who believe. For there is no distinction:

Luke 10:27 And he answered, "You shall love the Lord your God with all your heart and with all your soul and with all your strength and with all your mind, and your neighbor as yourself."

Proverbs 12:13 An evil man is ensnared by the transgression of his lips, but the righteous escapes from trouble.

Proverbs 28:13 Whoever conceals his transgressions will not prosper, but he who confesses and forsakes them will obtain mercy.

Psalm 90:8 You have set our iniquities before you, our secret sins in the light of your presence.

Exodus 34:7 keeping steadfast love for thousands, forgiving iniquity and transgression and sin, but who will by no means clear the guilty, visiting the iniquity of the fathers on the children and the children's children, to the third and the fourth generation."

2 Peter 3:9 The Lord is not slow to fulfill his promise as some count slowness, but is patient toward you, not wishing that any should perish, but that all should reach repentance.

Philippians 2:13 for it is God who works in you, both to will and to work for his good pleasure.

Philippians 3:12 Not that I have already obtained this or am already perfect, but I press on to make it my own, because Christ Jesus has made me his own.

Philippians 1:6 And I am sure of this, that he who began a good work in you will bring it to completion at the day of Jesus Christ.

1 Corinthians 2:10 these things God has revealed to us through the Spirit. For the Spirit searches everything, even the depths of God.

Colossians 1:9 And so, from the day we heard, we have not ceased to pray for you, asking that you may be filled with the knowledge of his will in all spiritual wisdom and understanding,

Colossians 1:10 so as to walk in a manner worthy of the Lord, fully pleasing to him, bearing fruit in every good work and increasing in the knowledge of God.

Colossians 1:11 May you be strengthened with all power, according to his glorious might, for all endurance and patience with joy,

Colossians 1:12 giving thanks to the Father, who has qualified you to share in the inheritance of the saints in light.

6

WHAT IS HEAVEN AND HELL?

When we think of heaven and hell, we often think of heaven as "up there" and hell as "down there."

Each person, when they die, will go to their eternal destination, and that will either be living with God, or away from God. At the very basic, heaven is life with God. Hell is life without God. But what is that life like? 1 Kings 22:19 / 2 Thess. 1:9

Let's look at hell first. We might tend to sugarcoat it, but hell will be a terrible place. It will feel as if one is constantly burning. The Bible tells of a rich man, who went to hell, and a poor man named Lazarus, who went to heaven. The man in hell (aka Hades) was in torment. He cried out and asked for mercy. He asked that Lazarus could be sent so he may dip the tip of his finger in water and cool off his tongue, for he was "in agony in this flame." In the end times, the devil will be in "the lake of fire and brimstone ...tormented day and night forever and ever." This torment is not pain on your body, but pain on your soul. Luke 16:23-24 / Rev. 20:10 / Rev. 19:20

Many joke, saying they are on their way to hell. Hell is not a joke. It is an eternal destination, full of pain and sorrow. Those who joke about it most likely don't believe there is a hell. But there is. Whenever you hear casual references to hell, replace the word "hell" with "torment". The popular rock song "Highway to Hell" becomes "Highway to Torment." For those who know hell is real, the seriousness of choices becomes more obvious. Matt. 13:50 / Mark 9:43 / Jude 1:7

A great chasm exists between heaven and hell, and no one will ever be able to pass between them. Those in hell regret the choice they made in life to ignore when God called them, when God gave them opportunities to make the choice. Luke 16:26 / 2 Cor. 6:2

For the Christian, heaven is our eventual home, and it will be our home for all of time. Heaven, and life with God, will be so spectacular we cannot even conceive it. We can only get a glimpse of it in our imagination, like John 14:2 / Isa. 25:8 / John 14:2

Rev. 7:16	one looking at a shadow of a spectacular work of art. What does this shadow we have reveal about our destiny in heaven?
Rev. 21:4-8	• There will be no more tears, no more pain, no more death.
	• We will have perfect comfort, perfect peace, perfect love.
	• We will all live in harmony. There won't be any need for a legal system.
	• We will be living comfortably. There will be plenty of space.
Luke 23:43 Rev. 21:18	• The environment will be majestic and spectacular. And, it will stay that way. It won't deteriorate.
	• We won't have fear or anger or contention.
Matt. 6:19 1 Cor. 2:9	• You may hardly notice all these great personal pleasures because you will see God in His splendor and magnificence, and will be marveling at Him.
Rev. 7:11	It's difficult to really compare heaven or hell to things we experience on earth. Hell will be beyond our imagination. And so will heaven.

Verses from this section:

1 Kings 22:19 And Micaiah said, "Therefore hear the word of the Lord: I saw the Lord sitting on his throne, and all the host of heaven standing beside him on his right hand and on his left;

2 Thessalonians 1:9 They will suffer the punishment of eternal destruction, away from the presence of the Lord and from the glory of his might,

Luke 16:23-24 and in Hades, being in torment, he lifted up his eyes and saw Abraham far off and Lazarus at his side. And he called out, 'Father Abraham, have mercy on me, and send Lazarus to dip the end of his finger in water and cool my tongue, for I am in anguish in this flame.'

Revelation 20:10 and the devil who had deceived them was thrown into the lake of fire and sulfur where the beast and the false prophet were, and they will be tormented day and night forever and ever.

Revelation 19:20 And the beast was captured, and with it the false prophet who in its presence had done the signs by which he deceived those who had received the mark of the beast and those who worshiped its image. These two were thrown alive into the lake of fire that burns with sulfur.

Matthew 13:50 and throw them into the fiery furnace. In that place there will be weeping and gnashing of teeth.

Mark 9:43 And if your hand causes you to sin, cut it off. It is better for you to enter life crippled than with two hands to go to hell, to the unquenchable fire.

Jude 1:7 just as Sodom and Gomorrah and the surrounding cities, which likewise indulged in sexual immorality and pursued unnatural desire, serve as an example by undergoing a punishment of eternal fire.

Luke 16:26 And besides all this, between us and you a great chasm has been fixed, in order that those who would pass from here to you may not be able, and none may cross from there to us.'

2 Corinthians 6:2 For he says, "In a favorable time I listened to you, and in a day of salvation I have helped you." Behold, now is the favorable time; behold, now is the day of salvation.

John 14:2 In my Father's house are many rooms. If it were not so, would I have told you that I go to prepare a place for you?

Isaiah 25:8 He will swallow up death forever; and the Lord God will wipe away tears from all faces, and the reproach of his people he will take away from all the earth, for the Lord has spoken.

John 14:2 In my Father's house are many rooms. If it were not so, would I have told you that I go to prepare a place for you?

Revelation 7:16 They shall hunger no more, neither thirst anymore; the sun shall not strike them, nor any scorching heat.

Revelation 21:4 He will wipe away every tear from their eyes, and death shall be no more, neither shall there be mourning, nor crying, nor pain anymore, for the former things have passed away."

Revelation 21:5 And he who was seated on the throne said, "Behold, I am making all things new." Also he said, "Write this down, for these words are trustworthy and true."

Revelation 21:6 And he said to me, "It is done! I am the Alpha and the Omega, the beginning and the end. To the thirsty I will give from the spring of the water of life without payment.

Revelation 21:7 The one who conquers will have this heritage, and I will be his God and he will be my son.

Revelation 21:8 But as for the cowardly, the faithless, the detestable, as for murderers, the sexually immoral, sorcerers, idolaters, and all liars, their portion will be in the lake that burns with fire and sulfur, which is the second death."

Luke 23:43 And he said to him, "Truly, I say to you, today you will be with me in paradise."

Revelation 21:18 The wall was built of jasper, while the city was pure gold, like clear glass.

Matthew 6:19 Do not lay up for yourselves treasures on earth, where moth and rust destroy and where thieves break in and steal

1 Corinthians 2:9 But, as it is written, "What no eye has seen, nor ear heard, nor the heart of man imagined, what God has prepared for those who love him"

Revelation 7:11 And all the angels were standing around the throne and around the elders and the four living creatures, and they fell on their faces before the throne and worshiped God,

7

WHO IS A CHRISTIAN?

A Christian is a person who is in the position where their sins are forgiven by God through faith in Jesus, who has a relationship with God, and who will be with God in eternity in heaven.

Jesus is the Messiah, the Christ, the One who enables people to become a Christian. Without Jesus, no one could ever be in the position of a Christian.

No one is born a Christian. If we follow in our state at birth, our only destination would be hell. At some point in a Christian's life, this person was destined for hell, but something happened—they accepted Jesus into their life and His offer of forgiveness of sins. That person is now destined for heaven. They have become a Christian.

A Christian is a person who has realized the position they are in as a sinner, who cannot make things right with God by themselves. They decide to turn away from their disobedience to God, their sin, and by faith accept the unique gift of Jesus' sacrifice for themself. They accept this gift by faith, offered by God for forgiveness of their sins. This receipt of God's gift enables the relationship with God, and sets the person's eternity to be in heaven. They truly believe what Jesus did for all people, and accept that for themself. In that process of accepting the gift, they admit Jesus is Lord of all, and they make Jesus Lord of their life. A "Lord" is a ruler, and they give Jesus rule over their life.

When you are given a Christmas present, there are many ways it can be given—through the mail, left at your home, delivered in person, etc. Essentially the gift becomes yours when you take it.

There are many ways God presents His offer of heaven, i.e., eternal life through Christ. The road for each

Col. 2:13
1 John 4:13
Rom. 6:23

John 20:31
John 14:6
Acts 4:12

Rom. 3:23
John 3:3
John 14:3

Eph. 2:12
Luke 13:3
Rom. 5:1
Eph. 2:8-9
Rom. 5:17

John 12:26
Rom. 1:1
1 Cor. 8:6

1 Tim. 2:4

Rom. 2:4	person is varied. Look back at your life, and see all the ways God has been working with you to draw you to Him.
	God works events in each person's life so every person has the opportunity to become a Christian. During each
2 Pet. 3:9 Rom. 1:20	person's life, God gives them chances to accept His gift. He makes Himself known to every person, so they are without excuse. Maybe God is giving you that chance right now.
1 John 2:23	There is only one road to heaven—through Jesus. You cannot reject Jesus Christ and be a Christian. You cannot reject Jesus Christ and have a relationship with God.
Isa. 45:22 Mark 16:16 John 3:3	The Bible uses different terms for Christians. A Christian is "saved"—rescued from hell, the eventual path every person would be on without what Jesus did. A Christian is "born again"—the moment you become a Christian is your spiritual birth, leading to life with God.
1 Cor. 6:19 Rom. 8:26 Heb. 2:4 1 Cor. 14:1,12	When you become a Christian, the Holy Spirit comes into your life, and dwells in you. He prays for you and works with you in many ways to enable you to live the life God wants you to live, if you allow Him to work in you. He has given special gifts to you, for you to use in ministering to others.
2 Cor. 5:17 Eph. 2:10 Phil. 1:6 1 Cor. 13:11	As a result, your life will change. It is clear in Scripture the evidence you are a Christian is a changed heart and life. But it is also clear that, while there are immediate changes taking place, it is also a lifelong road to become who God wants you to be.

Verses from this section:

Colossians 2:13 And you, who were dead in your trespasses and the uncircumcision of your flesh, God made alive together with him, having forgiven us all our trespasses,

1 John 4:13 By this we know that we abide in him and he in us, because he has given us of his Spirit.

Romans 6:23 For the wages of sin is death, but the free gift of God is eternal life in Christ Jesus our Lord.

John 20:31 but these are written so that you may believe that Jesus is the Christ, the Son of God, and that by believing you may have life in his name.

John 14:6 Jesus said to him, "I am the way, and the truth, and the life. No one comes to the Father except through me.

Acts 4:12 And there is salvation in no one else, for there is no other name under heaven given among men by which we must be saved."

Romans 3:23 for all have sinned and fall short of the glory of God,

John 3:3 Jesus answered him, "Truly, truly, I say to you, unless one is born again he cannot see the kingdom of God."

John 14:3 And if I go and prepare a place for you, I will come again and will take you to myself, that where I am you may be also.

Ephesians 2:12 remember that you were at that time separated from Christ, alienated from the commonwealth of Israel and strangers to the covenants of promise, having no hope and without God in the world.

Luke 13:3 No, I tell you; but unless you repent, you will all likewise perish.

Romans 5:1 Therefore, since we have been justified by faith, we have peace with God through our Lord Jesus Christ.

Ephesians 2:8-9 For by grace you have been saved through faith. And this is not your own doing; it is the gift of God, not a result of works, so that no one may boast.

Romans 5:17 For if, because of one man's trespass, death reigned through that one man, much more will those who receive the abundance of grace and the free gift of righteousness reign in life through the one man Jesus Christ.

John 12:26 If anyone serves me, he must follow me; and where I am, there will my servant be also. If anyone serves me, the Father will honor him.

Romans 1:1 Paul, a servant of Christ Jesus, called to be an apostle, set apart for the gospel of God,

1 Corinthians 8:6 yet for us there is one God, the Father, from whom are all things and for whom we exist, and one Lord, Jesus Christ, through whom are all things and through whom we exist.

1 Timothy 2:4 who desires all people to be saved and to come to the knowledge of the truth.

Romans 2:4 Or do you presume on the riches of his kindness and forbearance and patience, not knowing that God's kindness is meant to lead you to repentance?

2 Peter 3:9 The Lord is not slow to fulfill his promise as some count slowness, but is patient toward you, not wishing that any should perish, but that all should reach repentance.

Romans 1:20 For his invisible attributes, namely, his eternal power and divine nature, have been clearly perceived, ever since the creation of the world, in the things that have been made. So they are without excuse.

1 John 2:23 No one who denies the Son has the Father. Whoever confesses the Son has the Father also.

Isaiah 45:22 "Turn to me and be saved, all the ends of the earth! For I am God, and there is no other.

Mark 16:16 Whoever believes and is baptized will be saved, but whoever does not believe will be condemned.

John 3:3 Jesus answered him, "Truly, truly, I say to you, unless one is born again he cannot see the kingdom of God."

1 Corinthians 6:19 Or do you not know that your body is a temple of the Holy Spirit within you, whom you have from God? You are not your own,

Romans 8:26 Likewise the Spirit helps us in our weakness. For we do not know what to pray for as we ought, but the Spirit himself intercedes for us with groanings too deep for words.

Hebrews 2:4 while God also bore witness by signs and wonders and various miracles and by gifts of the Holy Spirit distributed according to his will.

1 Corinthians 14:1 Pursue love, and earnestly desire the spiritual gifts, especially that you may prophesy.

1 Corinthians 14:12 So with yourselves, since you are eager for manifestations of the Spirit, strive to excel in building up the church.

2 Corinthians 5:17 Therefore, if anyone is in Christ, he is a new creation. The old has passed away; behold, the new has come.

Ephesians 2:10 For we are his workmanship, created in Christ Jesus for good works, which God prepared beforehand, that we should walk in them.

Philippians 1:6 And I am sure of this, that he who began a good work in you will bring it to completion at the day of Jesus Christ.

1 Corinthians 13:11 When I was a child, I spoke like a child, I thought like a child, I reasoned like a child. When I became a man, I gave up childish ways.

8

WHO ARE ANGELS AND DEMONS?

When someone says a person is angelic, they probably mean they are nice. We see many images throughout history of angels in art, mostly looking like small children with wings. For many people, this is their view of angels, but angels are so much more than this.

Angels are beings in heaven with God, who were created by God, and were with God when the earth and universe was created. We know the names of some of the angels—Gabriel, Michael, and Lucifer. Before the universe was created, Lucifer rebelled against God and took one third of the angels with him, who now live in separation from God. These angels are now called demons. The fallen angel Lucifer is the devil, is also called Satan, and is the ruler of the demons.

Gen. 2:1
Job 38:4,7
Luke 1:19
Rev. 12:7
Isa. 14:12-14
Jude 1:6

Demons serve their leader Satan. Satan works to draw people into sin. Demons also work toward that aim. We cannot accurately say "the devil made me do it," because the devil or demons cannot force a person to sin. But the devil and his cohort of demons may likely have influenced the person toward sin. People are also drawn to sin just by their nature, but demons take advantage of that when they can.

1 Cor. 10:20
2 Pet. 2:4

2 Cor. 4:4

Another goal of demons is to torment people. Sometimes they do this by dwelling in a person, which we call demon-possessed. Satan had entered Judas, which began Judas' betrayal of Jesus. But most often demons torment by influencing people through their surroundings. Either way, they will take advantage of the situation for their purpose.

Mark 1:34
Luke 22:3

Satan and demons are restricted in that they cannot do anything God does not permit them to do. We see a good example of this in the discussion between God and Satan in the book of Job.

Job 1:9-12

Though demons seek bad things for people, angels seek good things. The angels' primary purpose is to support God and His interests. They are God's army. They are guided by God, and obediently serve Him.

Ps. 103:20

Heb. 13:2
Luke 16:22
Matt. 26:53
Heb. 13:2

Angels can appear as humans to help people. The Bible says you may spend time with angels and not even know it. But even if an angel is not visible, they can have conversations with people.

Gen. 19:1-2
Gen. 32:24,25,28
2 Kings 6:17
Matt. 1:20

Most of the time they are invisibly helping people, who are unaware of their presence. As they serve God's interests, they protect people, they draw them away from sin, they help built their character, and they help to reveal God to people. They also can be used by God to answer prayers.

2 Sam. 24:16

Angels may be given great powers by God, to carry out His will. They can be given enough power to destroy a city.

Luke 2:13-15

Angels are often found to be praising God, calling Him holy. They teach us not only how to serve God, but also how to worship Him.

Isa. 6:2
Ezek. 1:25
Matthew 28:3
Ezekiel 1:11
Mark 16:5

Angels can take many forms. They can look like people, but they also can take stunning forms. Several times people were shocked and afraid when they saw angels. They may even appear as we often see them in art, with wings.

Josh. 5:13-14

There is an ongoing unseen heavenly conflict taking place we often don't appreciate. Demons work with the devil to cause as much hurt and damage in our lives as they can, while angels work with God to our benefit. There are angels all around us. Thank God for how He uses angels in our lives.

Verses from this section:

Genesis 2:1 Thus the heavens and the earth were finished, and all the host of them.

Job 38:4 "Where were you when I laid the foundation of the earth? Tell me, if you have understanding.

Job 38:7 when the morning stars sang together and all the sons of God shouted for joy?

Luke 1:19 And the angel answered him, "I am Gabriel. I stand in the presence of God, and I was sent to speak to you and to bring you this good news.

Revelation 12:7 Now war arose in heaven, Michael and his angels fighting against the dragon. And the dragon and his angels fought back,

Isaiah 14:12 "How you are fallen from heaven, O Day Star, son of Dawn! How you are cut down to the ground, you who laid the nations low!

Isaiah 14:13 You said in your heart, 'I will ascend to heaven; above the stars of God I will set my throne on high; I will sit on the mount of assembly in the far reaches of the north;

Isaiah 14:14 I will ascend above the heights of the clouds; I will make myself like the Most High.'

Jude 1:6 And the angels who did not stay within their own position of authority, but left their proper dwelling, he has kept in eternal chains under gloomy darkness until the judgment of the great day—

1 Corinthians 10:20 No, I imply that what pagans sacrifice they offer to demons and not to God. I do not want you to be participants with demons.

2 Peter 2:4 For if God did not spare angels when they sinned, but cast them into hell and committed them to chains of gloomy darkness to be kept until the judgment;

2 Corinthians 4:4 In their case the god of this world has blinded the minds of the unbelievers, to keep them from seeing the light of the gospel of the glory of Christ, who is the image of God.

Mark 1:34 And he healed many who were sick with various diseases, and cast out many demons. And he would not permit the demons to speak, because they knew him.

Luke 22:3 Then Satan entered into Judas called Iscariot, who was of the number of the twelve.

Job 1:9-12 Then Satan answered the Lord and said, "Does Job fear God for no reason? Have you not put a hedge around him and his house and all that he has, on every side? You have blessed the work of his hands, and his possessions have increased in the land. But stretch out your hand and touch all that he has, and he will curse you to your face." And the Lord said to Satan, "Behold, all that he has is in your hand. Only against him do not stretch out your hand." So Satan went out from the presence of the Lord.

Psalm 103:20 Bless the Lord, O you his angels, you mighty ones who do his word, obeying the voice of his word!

Hebrews 13:2 Do not neglect to show hospitality to strangers, for thereby some have entertained angels unawares.

Luke 16:22 The poor man died and was carried by the angels to Abraham's side. The rich man also died and was buried,

Matthew 26:53 Do you think that I cannot appeal to my Father, and he will at once send me more than twelve legions of angels?

Hebrews 13:2 Do not neglect to show hospitality to strangers, for thereby some have entertained angels unawares.

Genesis 19:1-2 The two angels came to Sodom in the evening, and Lot was sitting in the gate of Sodom. When Lot saw them, he rose to meet them and bowed himself with his face to the earth and said, "My lords, please turn aside to your servant's house and spend the night and wash your feet. Then you may rise up early and go on your way." They said, "No; we will spend the night in the town square."

Genesis 32:24-25 And Jacob was left alone. And a man wrestled with him until the breaking of the day. When the man saw that he did not prevail against Jacob, he touched his hip socket, and Jacob's hip was put out of joint as he wrestled with him.

Genesis 32:28 Then he said, "Your name shall no longer be called Jacob, but Israel, for you have striven with God and with men, and have prevailed."

2 Kings 6:17 Then Elisha prayed and said, "O Lord, please open his eyes that he may see." So the Lord opened the eyes of the young man, and he saw, and behold, the mountain was full of horses and chariots of fire all around Elisha.

Matthew 1:20 But as he considered these things, behold, an angel of the Lord appeared to him in a dream, saying, "Joseph, son of David, do not fear to take Mary as your wife, for that which is conceived in her is from the Holy Spirit.

2 Samuel 24:16 And when the angel stretched out his hand toward Jerusalem to destroy it, the Lord relented from the calamity and said to the angel who was working destruction among the people, "It is enough; now stay your hand." And the angel of the Lord was by the threshing floor of Araunah the Jebusite.

Luke 2:13 And suddenly there was with the angel a multitude of the heavenly host praising God and saying,

Luke 2:14 "Glory to God in the highest, and on earth peace among those with whom he is pleased!"

Luke 2:15 When the angels went away from them into heaven, the shepherds said to one another, "Let us go over to Bethlehem and see this thing that has happened, which the Lord has made known to us."

Isaiah 6:2 Above him stood the seraphim. Each had six wings: with two he covered his face, and with two he covered his feet, and with two he flew.

Ezekiel 1:25 And there came a voice from above the expanse over their heads. When they stood still, they let down their wings.

Joshua 5:13 When Joshua was by Jericho, he lifted up his eyes and looked, and behold, a man was standing before him with his drawn sword in his hand. And Joshua went to him and said to him, "Are you for us, or for our adversaries?"

Matthew 28:3 His appearance was like lightning, and his clothing white as snow.

Ezekiel 1:11 Such were their faces. And their wings were spread out above. Each creature had two wings, each of which touched the wing of another, while two covered their bodies.

Mark 16:5 And entering the tomb, they saw a young man sitting on the right side, dressed in a white robe, and they were alarmed.

Joshua 5:14 And he said, "No; but I am the commander of the army of the Lord. Now I have come." And Joshua fell on his face to the earth and worshiped and said to him, "What does my lord say to his servant?"

9

WHO IS THE DEVIL?

<table>
<tr><td>Luke 10:18
Isa. 14:12
Matt. 12:24
Rev. 12:4</td><td>The devil's name is Lucifer. He is also known as Satan, or Beelzebub. He is an angel, and like all angels, is a being created by God. But, he chose to rebel against God, wanting to have power like God. In his rebellion, he took a third of the angels with him, who became demons. The</td></tr>
<tr><td>John 12:31
Jude 1:6</td><td>devil and the angels who rebelled with him are no longer referred to as angels, but as demons. The devil is the ruler of the demons.</td></tr>
<tr><td>Rev. 20:10</td><td>The devil is also the ruler of the earth. He has great power on the earth. It is his kingdom—albeit temporary. For when Jesus returns, the kingdom will be taken away from him.</td></tr>
<tr><td>Job 1:12
Job 1:7</td><td>The devil is subject to God, and can do nothing without God letting him. God has given him a lot of freedom to do as he pleases on the earth, but all his freedoms will disappear in the end times.</td></tr>
<tr><td>1 Sam. 16:14
Acts 19:15</td><td>Like each angel or demon, and unlike God, Jesus, and the Holy Spirit, the devil can only be in one place at one time, and can only focus on one thing at a time. It is rare that a person interacts with Satan himself. It is usually with his demons.</td></tr>
<tr><td>1 Pet. 5:8
Eph. 6:16</td><td>God cautions Christians to be wary of the devil and his demons. Their goal is to draw Christians away from God and toward sin, and to distract Christians as much as possible from their devotion to God.</td></tr>
<tr><td>Gal. 5:18
Gal. 5:25</td><td>Any time the devil can influence us to rebel against God, he will take that opportunity. He tried to pull Jesus away from God. Along with other temptations, he offered to Jesus three great temptations. These came when Jesus was at His weakest, after fasting for forty days. In the</td></tr>
<tr><td>Matt. 4:2-10</td><td>temptations he offered Jesus, we see the same temptations being placed in our lives. These were temptations for our own inappropriate desires and wants, temptations to</td></tr>
</table>

challenge God's work in our lives, and temptations to give us unhealthy power and greatness.

The good thing is the devil has no real power over Christians that God does not allow, and the Holy Spirit works with the spirit of Christians to guide them to do what God wants. | James 4:7
Gal. 5:22-23

In the end times, Satan will not be ruling over the earth or hell. He'll be tormented just like all the others who have rejected God.

Verses from this section:

Luke 10:18 And he said to them, "I saw Satan fall like lightning from heaven.

Isaiah 14:12 "How you are fallen from heaven, O Day Star, son of Dawn! How you are cut down to the ground, you who laid the nations low!

Matthew 12:24 But when the Pharisees heard it, they said, "It is only by Beelzebul, the prince of demons, that this man casts out demons."

Revelation 12:4 His tail swept down a third of the stars of heaven and cast them to the earth. And the dragon stood before the woman who was about to give birth, so that when she bore her child he might devour it.

John 12:31 Now is the judgment of this world; now will the ruler of this world be cast out.

Jude 1:6 And the angels who did not stay within their own position of authority, but left their proper dwelling, he has kept in eternal chains under gloomy darkness until the judgment of the great day—

Revelation 20:10 and the devil who had deceived them was thrown into the lake of fire and sulfur where the beast and the false prophet were, and they will be tormented day and night forever and ever.

Job 1:12 And the Lord said to Satan, "Behold, all that he has is in your hand. Only against him do not stretch out your hand." So Satan went out from the presence of the Lord.

Job 1:7 The Lord said to Satan, "From where have you come?" Satan answered the Lord and said, "From going to and fro on the earth, and from walking up and down on it."

1 Samuel 16:14 Now the Spirit of the Lord departed from Saul, and a harmful spirit from the Lord tormented him.

Acts 19:15 But the evil spirit answered them, "Jesus I know, and Paul I recognize, but who are you?"

1 Peter 5:8 Be sober-minded; be watchful. Your adversary the devil prowls around like a roaring lion, seeking someone to devour.

Ephesians 6:16 In all circumstances take up the shield of faith, with which you can extinguish all the flaming darts of the evil one;

Galatians 5:18 But if you are led by the Spirit, you are not under the law.

Galatians 5:25 If we live by the Spirit, let us also keep in step with the Spirit.

Matthew 4:2 And after fasting forty days and forty nights, he was hungry.

Matthew 4:3 And the tempter came and said to him, "If you are the Son of God, command these stones to become loaves of bread."

Matthew 4:4 But he answered, "It is written, "'Man shall not live by bread alone, but by every word that comes from the mouth of God.'"

Matthew 4:5 Then the devil took him to the holy city and set him on the pinnacle of the temple

Matthew 4:6 and said to him, "If you are the Son of God, throw yourself down, for it is written, "'He will command his angels concerning you,' and "'On their hands they will bear you up, lest you strike your foot against a stone.'"

Matthew 4:7 Jesus said to him, "Again it is written, 'You shall not put the Lord your God to the test.'"

Matthew 4:8 Again, the devil took him to a very high mountain and showed him all the kingdoms of the world and their glory.

Matthew 4:9 And he said to him, "All these I will give you, if you will fall down and worship me."

Matthew 4:10 Then Jesus said to him, "Be gone, Satan! For it is written, "'You shall worship the Lord your God and him only shall you serve.'"

James 4:7 Submit yourselves therefore to God. Resist the devil, and he will flee from you.

Galatians 5:22-23 But the fruit of the Spirit is love, joy, peace, patience, kindness, goodness, faithfulness, gentleness, self-control; against such things there is no law.

10

WHAT IS PRAYER?

Because God has placed as least a basic desire for Him in every person, it is a rare person who doesn't on occasion have a few words with God. We want to communicate with God, especially when we need Him. | Rom. 1:19 / Gen. 18:27

In any relationship, communication is essential for that relationship to grow. It's no different with our relationship with God. Prayer needs to be a regular part of that relationship. Jesus had a great relationship with God, and He often would go away by Himself to pray. If it was important in Jesus' relationship with God, it must be part of ours as well. | Acts 10:9 / James 4:8 / Luke 6:12

Prayer is essential, but how does one pray? The great thing is Jesus taught us how to pray. He said pray this way, when He gave us the Lord's Prayer, also called the Model Prayer. Jesus did not intend for us to repeat it word for word, but wanted us to understand the concepts of it, so we would know how to pray. That prayer included:

- Adoration and praise of God
- Looking forward to being with God
- Confessing and asking forgiveness of sins
- Asking help to avoid temptations
- Asking for things for us and others
  - Yet letting His will be done
- Asking for freedom from evil
- Acknowledging who God is

Matt. 6:9-13

Instead of only asking God for things, we need to lift Him up and praise Him, as Jesus did, and as angels were often seen doing. | Ps. 100:4

We need to make sure we thank Him for all things in our life, knowing He is working good in all things for us. | Rom. 8:32 / Jer. 29:11

Job 33:31-33
Ps. 85:8
Num. 9:8

Sometimes it is good to start prayer with silence, to realize God's presence, to get ready for your time together. During prayer, we need to pause, and listen, to see what God is saying to our spirit. He often can make you aware of what He wants in these quiet moments.

1 Thess. 5:18

We are also encouraged to start with thanksgiving, because it puts everything else in proper perspective.

Luke 18:1
Matt. 14:31

The best way to learn how to pray is to spend time in prayer. The more time you spend in prayer, the more you see God responding. This shows you over and over He does answer, and He is ready to help you. Answered prayer will remove unbelief and solidify your faith. Sometimes we don't know what to pray for, so ask God for guidance.

Mark 1:35

Prayer is challenging, especially since we are easily distracted. Prayer defeats the devil, so he will do everything possible to keep you from praying. You will notice how many distractions come when you attempt to pray. Push yourself to pray. Setting specifics times to pray helps with your focus.

Ps. 5:3

John 14:13-14
John 15:15
James 2:23

We should not worry about carefully crafting the words in our prayers. They do not have to be eloquent. God knows our hearts. The most important thing is we are coming to God and opening up to Him. He wants us to speak to Him as one speaks to a friend.

Heb. 11:6

Faith is important for prayer to be effectual. Trust God. Know God hears, and wants the best for us. God in His perfect wisdom knows what is best for us.

Ps. 116:4

God works to build our relationship with Him. God also works to build our character. These two things are His primary goals for us. In determining when and how to respond to our prayers, He is shaping these into our lives. God's answers to prayer are always with His agenda in mind. But, within that agenda, He loves to give us good things. He is our Father, and just like our human fathers, God loves to help us. He tells us to pray not just for our needs, but also for our desires.

Prov. 3:5-6

Matt. 7:11
Ps. 37:4

1 Thess. 5:17
Heb. 7:25

God asks us to always be praying. This means we should always be in communication with Him, aware of His presence, chatting with Him as you would a friend. As much as we can, we should pray about everything going on in our lives. As often as you can, draw yourself to Him.

In addition to our prayers, Jesus and the Holy Spirit are regularly praying for us, especially for things we don't even know we need.

Jesus' purpose was to show us God, and to bring us to God. When we pray to God, we are praying through Jesus, because He was the one who enabled us to be able to go to God. Without Jesus we cannot go to God. You don't have to say it, but when we pray, as Christians we know we are talking to God in Jesus' name. As part of our prayers to God, we should also thank Jesus for what He did, and honor Him.

Prayer can be by yourself, or with others. It can be within yourself, or you can speak it out loud. You can be in any position, but some think folding the hands, kneeling, and similar positions help you to focus on God when you pray. It can be eyes open or shut, in the middle of intense activities, or in perfect quietness.

The Bible tells us in some situations, God likes regular, persistent prayers. These prayers are not to be memorized or repetitive, ritual prayers, but prayers from the heart.

We know how important prayer is, yet we still neglect to pray. We miss out on great blessings. When we have struggles in our life, few ever suggest it is because of a lack of prayer. In counseling, you rarely hear advice that you need to pray more. Failures may be avoided with prayer. Prayer can accomplish great things. It is sad we have this solution, and yet we still neglect to pray.

For any sins you struggle with, prayer gives you a strong weapon against temptation. It is easy to fight these battles when you cover them in prayer. Confession admits the errors, and asking for forgiveness restores our relationship with God. But if you are hiding sin, or just ignoring it, sin can hinder your prayers. Praying with the wrong motives, like pride and selfishness, can hinder your prayers. Bitterness, anger, critical attitudes, and hatred can hinder your prayers. Lack of trying to obey God's commands will also block the effectiveness of your prayers.

Prayer is limitless —prayer can do anything God can do. Realize every answer to prayer is a miracle, that God has intervened, and something took place that otherwise would not have. For God, simple answers are just as easy

Rom. 8:26
John 17:20-21

John 14:6

John 5:23

Luke 5:16
Matt. 18:19-20

Luke 11:9
Dan. 10:2,12
James 4:2

1 Sam. 12:23

Matt. 6:13
1 John 1:9

John 3:20
Prov. 28:9
Ps. 66:18
Luke 18:10-14

John 15:7
1 John 5:14-15

Ps. 66:19
Ps. 118:21
Mark 11:24

Acts 6:4

as big answers. Pray for small things, but also pray for big things. The more we see answered prayers in small things, the more we will learn to trust God in the big things. We should look for God to surprise us. God loves to make Himself visible in your life.

Look around you for who to pray for. There are many people in need of our prayers, that are living with visible and hidden troubles. This includes those in leadership at our churches. We often don't think of their needs, but prayer is the most important activity in any ministry. Prayer is the most important activity in our lives.

God wants to hear our prayers. Like any parent, He longingly waits to hear us pour out our hearts about what is going on in our lives.

Here is some poignant advice on how to pray, from a French Roman Catholic Priest, Francois Fenelon, who lived in the seventeenth century:

> Tell God all that is in your heart, as one unloads one's heart, its pleasures and its pains, to a dear friend. Tell Him your troubles that He may comfort you; tell Him your joys, that He may sober them; tell Him your longings, that He may purify them; tell Him your dislikes, that He may help you to conquer them; talk to Him of your temptations, that He may shield you from them; show Him the wounds of your heart, that He may heal them; lay bear your indifference to good, your depraved tasted for evil, your instability. Tell Him how self-love makes you unjust to others, how vanity tempts you to be insincere, how pride disguises you to yourself as to others.

> If you thus pour out all your weaknesses, needs, and troubles, there will be no lack of what to say. You will never exhaust the subject. It is continually being renewed. People who have no secrets from each other never want for subjects of conversation. They do not weigh their words, for there is nothing to be held back; neither do they seek for something to say. They talk out of the abundance of the heart, without consideration, just what they think. Blessed are they

who attain to such familiar, unreserved conversation with God.

You have freedom for when and how to pray. Just do it. You'll get close to God as a result, and your faith will grow as you see God work in your life and in the lives of those around you.

Verses from this section:

Romans 1:19 For what can be known about God is plain to them, because God has shown it to them.

Genesis 18:27 Abraham answered and said, "Behold, I have undertaken to speak to the Lord, I who am but dust and ashes.

Acts 10:9 The next day, as they were on their journey and approaching the city, Peter went up on the housetop about the sixth hour to pray.

James 4:8 Draw near to God, and he will draw near to you. Cleanse your hands, you sinners, and purify your hearts, you double-minded.

Luke 6:12 In these days he went out to the mountain to pray, and all night he continued in prayer to God.

Matthew 6:9 Pray then like this: "Our Father in heaven, hallowed be your name.

Matthew 6:10 Your kingdom come, your will be done, on earth as it is in heaven.

Matthew 6:11 Give us this day our daily bread,

Matthew 6:12 and forgive us our debts, as we also have forgiven our debtors.

Matthew 6:13 And lead us not into temptation, but deliver us from evil.

Psalm 100:4 Enter his gates with thanksgiving, and his courts with praise! Give thanks to him; bless his name!

Romans 8:32 He who did not spare his own Son but gave him up for us all, how will he not also with him graciously give us all things?

Jeremiah 29:11 For I know the plans I have for you, declares the Lord, plans for welfare and not for evil, to give you a future and a hope.

Job 33:31-33 "Pay attention, O Job, listen to me; be silent, and I will speak. If you have any words, answer me; speak, for I desire to justify you. If not, listen to me; be silent, and I will teach you wisdom."

Psalm 85:8 Let me hear what God the Lord will speak, for he will speak peace to his people, to his saints; but let them not turn back to folly.

Numbers 9:8 And Moses said to them, "Wait, that I may hear what the Lord will command concerning you."

1 Thessalonians 5:18 give thanks in all circumstances; for this is the will of God in Christ Jesus for you.

Romans 8:26 Likewise the Spirit helps us in our weakness. For we do not know what to pray for as we ought, but the Spirit himself intercedes for us with groanings too deep for words.

Luke 18:1 And he told them a parable to the effect that they ought always to pray and not lose heart.

Matthew 14:31 Jesus immediately reached out his hand and took hold of him, saying to him, "O you of little faith, why did you doubt?"

Mark 1:35 And rising very early in the morning, while it was still dark, he departed and went out to a desolate place, and there he prayed.

Psalm 5:3 O Lord, in the morning you hear my voice; in the morning I prepare a sacrifice for you[a] and watch.

John 14:13-14 Whatever you ask in my name, this I will do, that the Father may be glorified in the Son. If you ask me anything in my name, I will do it.

John 15:15 No longer do I call you servants, for the servant does not know what his master is doing; but I have called you friends, for all that I have heard from my Father I have made known to you.

James 2:23 and the Scripture was fulfilled that says, "Abraham believed God, and it was counted to him as righteousness"—and he was called a friend of God.

Hebrews 11:6 And without faith it is impossible to please him, for whoever would draw near to God must believe that he exists and that he rewards those who seek him.

Psalm 116:4 Then I called on the name of the Lord: "O Lord, I pray, deliver my soul!"

Proverbs 3:5-6 Trust in the Lord with all your heart, and do not lean on your own understanding. In all your ways acknowledge him, and he will make straight your paths.

Matthew 7:11 If you then, who are evil, know how to give good gifts to your children, how much more will your Father who is in heaven give good things to those who ask him!

Psalm 37:4 Delight yourself in the Lord, and he will give you the desires of your heart.

1 Thessalonians 5:17 pray without ceasing,

Hebrews 7:25 Consequently, he is able to save to the uttermost those who draw near to God through him, since he always lives to make intercession for them.

John 17:20-21 "I do not ask for these only, but also for those who will believe in me through their word, 21 that they may all be one, just as you, Father, are in me, and I in you, that they also may be in us, so that the world may believe that you have sent me."

John 14:6 Jesus said to him, "I am the way, and the truth, and the life. No one comes to the Father except through me."

John 5:23 that all may honor the Son, just as they honor the Father. Whoever does not honor the Son does not honor the Father who sent him.

Luke 5:16 But he would withdraw to desolate places and pray.

Matthew 18:19-20 Again I say to you, if two of you agree on earth about anything they ask, it will be done for them by my Father in heaven. For where two or three are gathered in my name, there am I among them."

Luke 11:9 And I tell you, ask, and it will be given to you; seek, and you will find; knock, and it will be opened to you.

Daniel 10:2 In those days I, Daniel, was mourning for three weeks.

Daniel 10:12 Then he said to me, "Fear not, Daniel, for from the first day that you set your heart to understand and humbled yourself before your God, your words have been heard, and I have come because of your words.

James 4:2 You desire and do not have, so you murder. You covet and cannot obtain, so you fight and quarrel. You do not have, because you do not ask.

1 Samuel 12:23 Moreover, as for me, far be it from me that I should sin against the Lord by ceasing to pray for you, and I will instruct you in the good and the right way.

Matthew 6:13 And lead us not into temptation, but deliver us from evil.

1 John 1:9 If we confess our sins, he is faithful and just to forgive us our sins and to cleanse us from all unrighteousness.

John 3:20 For everyone who does wicked things hates the light and does not come to the light, lest his works should be exposed.

Proverbs 28:9 If one turns away his ear from hearing the law, even his prayer is an abomination.

Psalm 66:18 If I had cherished iniquity in my heart, the Lord would not have listened.

Luke 18:10 "Two men went up into the temple to pray, one a Pharisee and the other a tax collector.

Luke 18:11 The Pharisee, standing by himself, prayed thus: 'God, I thank you that I am not like other men, extortioners, unjust, adulterers, or even like this tax collector.

Luke 18:12 I fast twice a week; I give tithes of all that I get.'

Luke 18:13 But the tax collector, standing far off, would not even lift up his eyes to heaven, but beat his breast, saying, 'God, be merciful to me, a sinner!'

Luke 18:14 I tell you, this man went down to his house justified, rather than the other. For everyone who exalts himself will be humbled, but the one who humbles himself will be exalted."

John 15:7 If you abide in me, and my words abide in you, ask whatever you wish, and it will be done for you.

1 John 5:14-15 And this is the confidence that we have toward him, that if we ask anything according to his will he hears us. And if we know that he hears us in whatever we ask, we know that we have the requests that we have asked of him.

Psalm 66:19 But truly God has listened; he has attended to the voice of my prayer.

Psalm 118:21 I thank you that you have answered me and have become my salvation.

Mark 11:24 Therefore I tell you, whatever you ask in prayer, believe that you have received it, and it will be yours.

Acts 6:4 But we will devote ourselves to prayer and to the ministry of the word.

11

TELL ME ABOUT OBEYING GOD

There is no better place to be in life than when you are doing the things God wants you to do. This is much more than just avoiding sin. It is doing what God wants you to do and going where God wants you to go. | 1 Sam. 15:22 / Mic. 6:8

Let's say a parent wants a child to do a chore. The parent is not asking the child to avoid doing wrong things like lying or stealing. The parent wants the child to be part of what they are doing, and where they are going, in taking care of their house. If the child ignores requests of the parent, how that hurts. But what joy to the parent when the child not only does it, but with a great attitude. And, even better, asks how to help! | Col. 3:23 / Ps. 51:16-17 / Mic. 7:18 / Matt. 6:33

Our heart needs to be ready and available to obey God. The Bible tells us God delights in our obedience, and how much more so when we are seeking it, and ready for it. | Ps. 68:3

Avoiding sin is a huge part of obeying God, and critical for a good relationship with Him. We need to understand we cannot just accept the fact that we will sin—we need to push for excellence. When you take a test, do you give up because you cannot get 100 percent? Does a basketball player give up because they can't make every shot? God wants to see our desire to avoid sin, to fight hard, to run this race with endurance. | Rom. 6:15 / 1 Cor. 9:24 / Heb. 12:1 / 2 Tim. 4:7 / Phil. 3:14

This excellence means looking for how to obey God. You should wake up each day asking God what He would have you do that day. And then listen, watch, pay attention, and see where God leads you. He may speak to you through the Bible, through prayer, through circumstances, etc. When you pray, try to listen to what the Holy Spirit is telling your spirit. | Luke 9:23 / Acts 17:11 / John 5:39 / 1 Cor. 15:31

Sometimes listening to God and obeying God is a scary thing. When the Israelites were getting ready to cross | Num. 13:30-31

	the Jordan River into the Promised Land, it was scary—
2 Tim. 1:7	ten of the twelve scouts said don't go! The demons will
	tell you reasons for not obeying, and much of that is based
Phil. 4:13	on fear. The great thing about obeying God is that, when
John 15:16	He asks you to do something, He will support your
	efforts, especially when it's something beyond where you
Exod. 4:10	normally go, like when He made Moses into the leader he
	became, even though he was a man who could not speak
	well.
Ps. 46:10	Take some quiet time with God. Reflect, pause, listen,
Ps. 1:2	pray, read, watch. See where God leads you.
	And then, obey.

Verses from this section:

1 Samuel 15:22 And Samuel said, "Has the Lord as great delight in burnt offerings and sacrifices, as in obeying the voice of the Lord? Behold, to obey is better than sacrifice, and to listen than the fat of rams.

Micah 6:8 He has told you, O man, what is good; and what does the Lord require of you but to do justice, and to love kindness, and to walk humbly with your God?

Colossians 3:23 Whatever you do, work heartily, as for the Lord and not for men,

Psalm 51:16-17 For you will not delight in sacrifice, or I would give it; you will not be pleased with a burnt offering. The sacrifices of God are a broken spirit; a broken and contrite heart, O God, you will not despise.

Micah 7:18 Who is a God like you, pardoning iniquity and passing over transgression for the remnant of his inheritance? He does not retain his anger forever, because he delights in steadfast love.

Matthew 6:33 But seek first the kingdom of God and his righteousness, and all these things will be added to you.

Psalm 68:3 But the righteous shall be glad; they shall exult before God; they shall be jubilant with joy!

Romans 6:15 What then? Are we to sin because we are not under law but under grace? By no means!

1 Corinthians 9:24 Do you not know that in a race all the runners run, but only one receives the prize? So run that you may obtain it.

Hebrews 12:1 Therefore, since we are surrounded by so great a cloud of witnesses, let us also lay aside every weight, and sin which clings so closely, and let us run with endurance the race that is set before us,

2 Timothy 4:7 I have fought the good fight, I have finished the race, I have kept the faith.

Philippians 3:14 I press on toward the goal for the prize of the upward call of God in Christ Jesus.

Luke 9:23 And he said to all, "If anyone would come after me, let him deny himself and take up his cross daily and follow me.

Acts 17:11 Now these Jews were more noble than those in Thessalonica; they received the word with all eagerness, examining the Scriptures daily to see if these things were so.

John 5:39 You search the Scriptures because you think that in them you have eternal life; and it is they that bear witness about me,

1 Corinthians 15:31 I protest, brothers, by my pride in you, which I have in Christ Jesus our Lord, I die every day!

Numbers 13:30 But Caleb quieted the people before Moses and said, "Let us go up at once and occupy it, for we are well able to overcome it."

Numbers 13:31 Then the men who had gone up with him said, "We are not able to go up against the people, for they are stronger than we are."

2 Timothy 1:7 for God gave us a spirit not of fear but of power and love and self-control.

Philippians 4:13 I can do all things through him who strengthens me.

John 15:16 You did not choose me, but I chose you and appointed you that you should go and bear fruit and that your fruit should abide, so that whatever you ask the Father in my name, he may give it to you.

Exodus 4:10 But Moses said to the Lord, "Oh, my Lord, I am not eloquent, either in the past or since you have spoken to your servant, but I am slow of speech and of tongue."

Psalm 46:10 "Be still, and know that I am God. I will be exalted among the nations, I will be exalted in the earth!"

Psalm 1:2 but his delight is in the law of the Lord, and on his law he meditates day and night.

12

TELL ME ABOUT CHURCH

Acts 11:22
Rev. 2:1
Acts 9:31
Eph. 3:10

When people talk about a church, they typically refer to a group of co-located Christians who get together in a particular building, to preach, fellowship, worship, pray, serve the community, etc. The Bible mentions several specific churches, like the churches in Jerusalem, in Ephesus, in Philippi, and in Colossae.

1 Cor. 15:9
Matt. 16:18
Eph. 1:22
Col. 1:18

The Bible also talks about another church—the collective group of Christians worldwide. This is simply called "the church," and is referenced whenever it discusses universal principles that apply to all churches or believers. Christ is the head of the church. The church at that time was growing, but was also undergoing persecution. Today we can talk about the church, and what is going on with Christians around the world.

Most of the time, a local church contains a particular group of Christians belonging to the same denomination. A denomination is a collection of believers, and churches, who have relatively the same beliefs and origins. Some denominations have been started by famous Christians like Martin Luther and John Calvin. There are some very large denominations, and some small ones.

There are several ways in which denominations may differ. It may be how music is played, how baptism is performed, how the worship is run, etc. Denominations will also differ in some complex Biblical concepts, like the end times, predestination, baptism, and eternal security.

John 14:6
Acts 4:12

The important factors the determine what a Christian church is versus what a cult is, are the church's view of God, Jesus, the Holy Spirit, salvation, and the Bible. These are the foundational doctrines where if a church strays from the truths taught in the Bible on these subjects. That kind of church should be avoided.

Denominations typically have a central body that governs, to some extent, statements of belief, church operations and hierarchy, and general collective funds for missionaries and other broad services.

Biblically, we are given a lot of freedom on how churches are organized. You will see a lot of differences between them. Some are closely tied to a denomination, whereas others are more independent. Some have musical instruments, and some do not. Some are formal, and others are more casual. Churches can meet in homes or in official church buildings, or in just about any location. Regardless, the critical factors are what they teach on the foundational doctrines.

Acts 2:46

There is a lot of freedom on how the personnel in churches can be organized. Some churches have pastors, some don't—and the same for elders, deacons, and other offices.

Eph. 4:11
James 5:14
1 Tim. 3:10

Attending church is important because of our need to spend time with other believers, in worship, fellowship, and prayer.

Heb. 10:24-25
Acts 2:42

We attend services together called worship services. Everything done in these services is meant to lift up God—the music, the prayers, the offering, the sermon. These are to glorify God, and the church enables believers to do that together.

The Bible makes it clear we are not to be alone. It is very difficult to grow and mature in our walk with God when doing it by yourself. We need the support of others. They pray for you, encourage you, counsel you, and become your friends.

Church should be an important part of every Christian's life. Make sure you find a good, Biblical-based church, and attend regularly. Get involved with the activities and the people. You will grow in your walk with God, and you will see growth in others as well.

Verses from this section:

Acts 11:22 The report of this came to the ears of the church in Jerusalem, and they sent Barnabas to Antioch.

Revelation 2:1 "To the angel of the church in Ephesus write: 'The words of him who holds the seven stars in his right hand, who walks among the seven golden lampstands.

Acts 9:31 So the church throughout all Judea and Galilee and Samaria had peace and was being built up. And walking in the fear of the Lord and in the comfort of the Holy Spirit, it multiplied.

Ephesians 3:10 so that through the church the manifold wisdom of God might now be made known to the rulers and authorities in the heavenly places.

1 Corinthians 15:9 For I am the least of the apostles, unworthy to be called an apostle, because I persecuted the church of God.

Matthew 16:18 And I tell you, you are Peter, and on this rock I will build my church, and the gates of hell[b] shall not prevail against it.

Ephesians 1:22 And he put all things under his feet and gave him as head over all things to the church

Colossians 1:18 And he is the head of the body, the church. He is the beginning, the firstborn from the dead, that in everything he might be preeminent.

John 14:6 Jesus said to him, "I am the way, and the truth, and the life. No one comes to the Father except through me.

Acts 4:12 And there is salvation in no one else, for there is no other name under heaven given among men by which we must be saved."

Acts 2:46 And day by day, attending the temple together and breaking bread in their homes, they received their food with glad and generous hearts,

Ephesians 4:11 And he gave the apostles, the prophets, the evangelists, the shepherds and teachers,

James 5:14 Is anyone among you sick? Let him call for the elders of the church, and let them pray over him, anointing him with oil in the name of the Lord.

1 Timothy 3:10 And let them also be tested first; then let them serve as deacons if they prove themselves blameless.

Hebrews 10:24-25 And let us consider how to stir up one another to love and good works, not neglecting to meet together, as is the habit of some, but encouraging one another, and all the more as you see the Day drawing near.

Acts 2:42 And they devoted themselves to the apostles' teaching and the fellowship, to the breaking of bread and the prayers.

13

WHAT IS BAPTISM?

Jesus, during His last hours physically on the earth, gave us what is called the Great Commission, telling His followers to go to all the nations of the earth, teaching about Him, and baptizing each new disciple.

Matt. 28:19-20

In the book of Acts, which is the history of the early church immediately after Jesus' ascension, we read about people converting to Christianity. In each case, the person was immediately baptized.

Acts 2:41
Acts 16:31-33
Acts 18:8

Baptism is coupled with a person's conversion to become a Christian. It is a statement or proclamation to the world of a person's decision to accept Christ and become a Christian. And, it is a commandment from Christ—Christians are to be baptized. Anyone who neglects or refuses to become baptized is not doing what God wants. If you have committed your life to Christ, you need to be baptized to have a healthy relationship with God.

Luke 3:21
Mark 16:16

In some ways it is like a marriage certificate—it is your declaration of your state as a Christian.

In addition to the statement baptism makes to others, it also is how we identify with what Jesus did. Baptism is a picture of His death, burial, and resurrection. We die to our sins, we bury them, and because of Jesus, we rise into a new, forgiven life. Baptism not only shows what Jesus did, but it also shows what has happened to us.

Rom. 6:4-7

2 Cor. 5:17

For those who convert to Christianity from other religions, often it is the act of baptism that is the defining moment of the conversion because it declares to others you are leaving behind the old beliefs just as much as it declares your acceptance of new beliefs.

Each church will baptize using one of three different methods to baptize—sprinkle water, pour water, or immerse (dip) in water. There are many theological

Eph. 4:5
1 Cor. 12:13
Gal. 3:27

arguments about which method the early church practiced and which is the proper way to baptize. Regardless of how it is performed, the important thing is that you follow Christ's command to be baptized, that you align with Christ by your declaration via baptism.

Some churches believe baptism is a required part of the conversion to Christianity, and that you cannot become a Christian until you follow your faith decision with the act of baptism. Regardless, it is a commandment of Christ, so each person placing their faith in Christ for forgiveness and salvation should obey Him by being baptized.

Acts 8:38
Acts 16:15

Who can baptize? Any Christian can baptize. There are no biblical restrictions on who can baptize, other than it needs to be a believer. Some churches may have restrictions within their church, but there are no biblical restrictions.

Where should a baptism take place? Anywhere there is water. There are no biblical restrictions as to where.

Acts 8:36

Our reaction, when we learn of God's desire for us to be baptized, should be like the Ethiopian official who Philip had just shared Christ with. When seeing water, he exclaimed, "Look! Water! What prevents me from being baptized?"

When should you be baptized? When you place your faith in Christ for salvation, or soon afterwards. The biblical examples in Acts always show baptisms when the person becomes a Christian. It is common in some churches for baptisms to be scheduled, because it is a special event, to allow family members and friends to be present during it.

If you are a Christian and have been waiting to be baptized, now is the time. You don't need a deep understanding—you only need to know it is what God wants you to do.

Verses from this section:

Matthew 28:19-20 Go therefore and make disciples of all nations, baptizing them in the name of the Father and of the Son and of the Holy Spirit, teaching them to observe all that I have commanded you. And behold, I am with you always, to the end of the age."

Acts 2:41 So those who received his word were baptized, and there were added that day about three thousand souls.

Acts 16:31 And they said, "Believe in the Lord Jesus, and you will be saved, you and your household."

Acts 16:32 And they spoke the word of the Lord to him and to all who were in his house.

Acts 16:33 And he took them the same hour of the night and washed their wounds; and he was baptized at once, he and all his family.

Acts 18:8 Crispus, the ruler of the synagogue, believed in the Lord, together with his entire household. And many of the Corinthians hearing Paul believed and were baptized.

Luke 3:21 Now when all the people were baptized, and when Jesus also had been baptized and was praying, the heavens were opened,

Mark 16:16 Whoever believes and is baptized will be saved, but whoever does not believe will be condemned.

Romans 6:4 We were buried therefore with him by baptism into death, in order that, just as Christ was raised from the dead by the glory of the Father, we too might walk in newness of life.

Romans 6:5 For if we have been united with him in a death like his, we shall certainly be united with him in a resurrection like his.

Romans 6:6 We know that our old self was crucified with him in order that the body of sin might be brought to nothing, so that we would no longer be enslaved to sin.

Romans 6:7 For one who has died has been set free from sin.

2 Corinthians 5:17 Therefore, if anyone is in Christ, he is a new creation. The old has passed away; behold, the new has come.

Ephesians 4:5 one Lord, one faith, one baptism,

1 Corinthians 12:13 For in one Spirit we were all baptized into one body— Jews or Greeks, slaves or free—and all were made to drink of one Spirit.

Galatians 3:27 For as many of you as were baptized into Christ have put on Christ.

Acts 8:38 And he commanded the chariot to stop, and they both went down into the water, Philip and the eunuch, and he baptized him.

Acts 16:15 And after she was baptized, and her household as well, she urged us, saying, "If you have judged me to be faithful to the Lord, come to my house and stay." And she prevailed upon us.

Acts 8:36 And as they were going along the road they came to some water, and the eunuch said, "See, here is water! What prevents me from being baptized?"

14

WHAT IS COMMUNION?

Leonardo da Vinci's famous painting, The Last Supper, depicts Jesus with His twelve apostles at His last meal before His arrest and eventual crucifixion. Several important events took place during the meal. At that meal Jesus established the practice of communion.

Matt. 26:20

During that meal, Jesus took some bread, and gave it to the others, telling them to "Take, eat; this is My body." After that, He gave them a cup containing "fruit of the vine," telling them "Drink from it, all of you; for this is My blood of the covenant, which is poured out for many for forgiveness of sins."

Matt. 26:26-28

During that meal, Jesus was not actually giving them His body and blood, as it was still intact—they were symbolic of what He was about to do, give His body and blood for the forgiveness of sins for all mankind.

He had asked them to eat the bread and drink the juice, to "do this in remembrance of Me" in the future. Jesus had asked them, after He ascended, to remember Him by doing the same.

Heb. 10:10
1 Pet. 3:18

Communion is the term for when Christians remember what Jesus did, by partaking in the eating of unfermented bread and drink. Sometimes the Bible refers to it as the "breaking of bread."

Luke 22:19

It is to be a solemn time, reflecting on what Jesus did for us, and also a time of self-evaluation, looking at your current walk with God, repenting of sin, and focusing on God. It is good to be quiet with God, and spend time in prayer, before taking communion.

Acts 2:42
1 Cor. 11:26-29

There are no restrictions as to when or where or how often you can take communion. Some churches take it every week because the early church did. You can do communion in your home.

Acts 20:7

Because the meal with Jesus and his apostles took place during the Jewish Passover festival, both the bread and drink were unfermented. This would mean the bread was unleavened (no yeast), and the drink was either a fruit drink (no alcohol) or a special kind of wine made from grapes dried before fermentation. Nowadays, because fruit juice is cheaper and much easier to obtain than unfermented wine, fruit juice is typically used for communion.

Churches supply the bread and drink in different ways. Some break the bread ahead of time, so when you eat, you select a piece of bread. At other places, you break the bread yourself. For the drink, some distribute individual tiny cups with the juice, whereas others (not as common) share a cup.

However you do it, Jesus asked that we remember Him with communion. May it be a time of prayer and self-reflection, and a time to draw close to Jesus, whenever you do it.

John 6:35

Verses from this section:

Matthew 26:20 When it was evening, he reclined at table with the twelve.

Matthew 26:26 Now as they were eating, Jesus took bread, and after blessing it broke it and gave it to the disciples, and said, "Take, eat; this is my body."

Matthew 26:27 And he took a cup, and when he had given thanks he gave it to them, saying, "Drink of it, all of you,

Matthew 26:28 for this is my blood of the covenant, which is poured out for many for the forgiveness of sins.

Hebrews 10:10 And by that will we have been sanctified through the offering of the body of Jesus Christ once for all.

1 Peter 3:18 For Christ also suffered once for sins, the righteous for the unrighteous, that he might bring us to God, being put to death in the flesh but made alive in the spirit,

Luke 22:19 And he took bread, and when he had given thanks, he broke it and gave it to them, saying, "This is my body, which is given for you. Do this in remembrance of me."

Acts 2:42 And they devoted themselves to the apostles' teaching and the fellowship, to the breaking of bread and the prayers.

1 Corinthians 11:26 For as often as you eat this bread and drink the cup, you proclaim the Lord's death until he comes.

1 Corinthians 11:27 Whoever, therefore, eats the bread or drinks the cup of the Lord in an unworthy manner will be guilty concerning the body and blood of the Lord.

1 Corinthians 11:28 Let a person examine himself, then, and so eat of the bread and drink of the cup.

1 Corinthians 11:29 For anyone who eats and drinks without discerning the body eats and drinks judgment on himself.

Acts 20:7 On the first day of the week, when we were gathered together to break bread, Paul talked with them, intending to depart on the next day, and he prolonged his speech until midnight.

John 6:35 Jesus said to them, "I am the bread of life; whoever comes to me shall not hunger, and whoever believes in me shall never thirst.

15

WHAT DOES GOD THINK OF MONEY?

Luke 12:15
Eccles. 5:10
James 3:16

Jesus once warned us, "Beware! Guard against every kind of greed. Life is not measured by how much you own." Greed is a consuming desire to always want more or better than you have now. Covetousness is looking at what others have with a passion to get it for yourself.

How do people view money? Someone once asked John D. Rockefeller how much money was enough. "One dollar more," he replied. The love of money is insatiable—it will never be quenched.

2 Pet. 2:14
Prov. 11:6
Luke 12:15

Ivan Boesky, at a graduation ceremony at a major university, declared "Greed is all right. I want you to know I think greed is healthy. You can be greedy and still feel good about yourself." *Newsweek* later commented, "The strangest thing when we look back will not be just that Ivan Boesky could say that at a business school graduation, but that it was greeted with laughter and applause."

Eccles. 6:7

People have many possessions, but they always seem to want more.

Matt. 6:21
Prov. 13:11
Heb. 13:5

The important factor for God is not how much money we have, but what is our view of money. We miss the point if we see covetousness as an issue of amount, not attitude. The poorest can be greedy; the richest can avoid greed. God wants us to have the proper attitude toward money no matter what financial state we are in.

2 Tim. 1:14
1 Tim. 6:20
1 Cor. 6:19-
20

We should view all our money as belonging to God, and view it as if we are managing it for God.

It is okay to want more and work for more, but the issue is where is our passion.

Here are some principles God wants us to have regarding money:

- Part of the purpose for earning money is so we can help others. Do you go to work with this goal in mind? — Eph. 4:28
- Tithing means "tenth". It is giving 10 percent of what you earn to God's causes, like the church. Tithing is not required in the New Testament, but God shows us it is a good principle to give at least that amount. — Mal. 3:8,10
- We should give wisely, since we are in effect stewards of the money God has allowed us to have. — James 2:15-16
- We should give quietly. We should not tell others how much we give. — Matt. 6:2-4 / Prov. 13:16
- We should spend wisely. We are not only stewards of what we give, but we are stewards in how we spend it for ourselves.
- When we lend to others, we should not expect anything in return. — Luke 6:34-35
  o It is okay to borrow and lend in business contracts, like mortgages, but proceed with wisdom and counsel.
- We should try to avoid debt. God tells us the borrower becomes the lender's slave, and it is a burden to carry debt. — Rom. 13:8 / Prov. 22:7
- When we give, it should be cheerfully, not begrudgingly. — 2 Cor. 9:6-7
- Giving is an act of worship. When you give, do it to praise and honor God.
- We should avoid gambling to make money (e.g., fantasy football is okay, for fun, not with the main goal of making money). — Prov. 13:11 / Hab. 2:7

Having a concern and passion for money or things that exceeds your love and passion for God will only cause problems in your life. For example, displaced desires for money and things is one of the central causes for marital strife. — 1 Tim. 6:10 / Rev. 3:17

Matt. 6:24 | The critical thing is where are our passions? What excites us? What do we spend most of our time dwelling on? The things of God or our own possessions?

Verses from this section:

Luke 12:15 And he said to them, "Take care, and be on your guard against all covetousness, for one's life does not consist in the abundance of his possessions."

Eccl 5:10 He who loves money will not be satisfied with money, nor he who loves wealth with his income; this also is vanity.

James 3:16 For where jealousy and selfish ambition exist, there will be disorder and every vile practice.

2 Peter 2:14 They have eyes full of adultery, insatiable for sin. They entice unsteady souls. They have hearts trained in greed. Accursed children!

Proverbs 11:6 The righteousness of the upright delivers them, but the treacherous are taken captive by their lust.

Luke 12:15 And he said to them, "Take care, and be on your guard against all covetousness, for one's life does not consist in the abundance of his possessions."

Eccl 6:7 All the toil of man is for his mouth, yet his appetite is not satisfied.

Matthew 6:21 For where your treasure is, there your heart will be also.

Proverbs 13:11 Wealth gained hastily will dwindle, but whoever gathers little by little will increase it.

Hebrews 13:5 Keep your life free from love of money, and be content with what you have, for he has said, "I will never leave you nor forsake you."

2 Timothy 1:14 By the Holy Spirit who dwells within us, guard the good deposit entrusted to you.

1 Timothy 6:20 O Timothy, guard the deposit entrusted to you. Avoid the irreverent babble and contradictions of what is falsely called "knowledge,"

1 Corinthians 6:19-20 Or do you not know that your body is a temple of the Holy Spirit within you, whom you have from God? You are not your own, for you were bought with a price. So glorify God in your body.

Ephesians 4:28 Let the thief no longer steal, but rather let him labor, doing honest work with his own hands, so that he may have something to share with anyone in need.

Malachi 3:8 Will man rob God? Yet you are robbing me. But you say, 'How have we robbed you?' In your tithes and contributions.

Malachi 3:9-10 You are cursed with a curse, for you are robbing me, the whole nation of you. Bring the full tithe into the storehouse, that there may be food in my house. And thereby put me to the test, says the Lord of hosts, if I will not open the windows of heaven for you and pour down for you a blessing until there is no more need.

James 2:15-16 If a brother or sister is poorly clothed and lacking in daily food, and one of you says to them, "Go in peace, be warmed and filled," without giving them the things needed for the body, what good is that?

Matthew 6:2 "Thus, when you give to the needy, sound no trumpet before you, as the hypocrites do in the synagogues and in the streets, that they may be praised by others. Truly, I say to you, they have received their reward.

Matthew 6:3 But when you give to the needy, do not let your left hand know what your right hand is doing,

Matthew 6:4 so that your giving may be in secret. And your Father who sees in secret will reward you.

Proverbs 13:16 In everything the prudent acts with knowledge, but a fool flaunts his folly.

Luke 6:34-35 And if you lend to those from whom you expect to receive, what credit is that to you? Even sinners lend to sinners, to get back the same amount. But love your enemies, and do good, and lend, expecting nothing in return, and your reward will be great, and you will be sons of the Most High, for he is kind to the ungrateful and the evil.

Romans 13:8 Owe no one anything, except to love each other, for the one who loves another has fulfilled the law.

Proverbs 22:7 The rich rules over the poor, and the borrower is the slave of the lender.

2 Corinthians 9:6-7 The point is this: whoever sows sparingly will also reap sparingly, and whoever sows bountifully will also reap bountifully. Each one must give as he has decided in his heart, not reluctantly or under compulsion, for God loves a cheerful giver.

Proverbs 13:11 Wealth gained hastily will dwindle, but whoever gathers little by little will increase it.

Habakkuk 2:7 Will not your debtors suddenly arise, and those awake who will make you tremble? Then you will be spoil for them.

1 Timothy 6:10 For the love of money is a root of all kinds of evils. It is through this craving that some have wandered away from the faith and pierced themselves with many pangs.

Revelation 3:17 For you say, I am rich, I have prospered, and I need nothing, not realizing that you are wretched, pitiable, poor, blind, and naked.

Matthew 6:24 "No one can serve two masters, for either he will hate the one and love the other, or he will be devoted to the one and despise the other. You cannot serve God and money.

16

TELL ME ABOUT LOVE

We see throughout the Bible God's desire for us is to be more like Him. But there are many laws and rules and commandments, how could we ever hope to get close to what He wants for us?

Jesus was once asked, "Teacher, which is the great commandment in the Law?" He replied, saying "'You shall love the lord your God with all your heart, and with all your soul, and with all your mind.' This is the great and foremost commandment. The second is like it, 'You shall love your neighbor as yourself.' On these two commandments depend the whole Law and the Prophets." Matt. 22:36-40

Instead of focusing on all the things you need to avoid, focus on loving God and others the way Jesus described—with all your heart. Instead of trying to deal with anger, greed, lust, bitterness, etc., if we can love in those situations the way God does, we will win those battles over sin. 1 John 2:10 / 1 Pet. 1:22

Of course, loving others as God does is not easy, but at least we can understand what our real goal is. He gave us, in 1 Corinthians 13, some clear guidelines, which includes patience, kindness, humility, focusing on truth, bearing with others, etc. This is how God wants us to interact with others. We should do nothing from selfishness, but we should always be looking out for the interests of others, regarding them as more important than ourselves. It is okay to look out for our own interests, but we should also be paying attention to the needs of others. And this includes every single person. We need to be careful not to exclude anyone. 1 Cor. 13:4-7 / Phil. 2:3-4 / 1 Tim. 2:4

There are three uses of love in the Bible—godly love, brotherly love, and sexual love. Jesus, in the passages mentioned above, was telling us about godly love. This is when we care for others the same way God does. Godly love is not just the best way to do what God wants. What God is telling us is if we love Him and others as He loves, with godly love, we will be doing exactly as God wants. When you are loving this way, there is no sin. It's not just the greatest commandment—ALL other commandments can be summed up in this one.

Brotherly love is the love we have for others as if they were part of our family. This is the affection we have for our friends. People we love this way are those we want to hang out with, our companions.

Sexual love is the passion with have for another person. This is what gets our heart beating faster. Sexual love is what motivates us to date and find a spouse. We need to be careful that we don't take these passions physically and mentally where we should not go. When married, our sexual love should be funneled to our spouse and no one else. Sexual love is not sin, unless it is misdirected sexual love.

The commandments can simply be summed up in telling us to love God and others with godly love. But, what does godly love look like? It is paying for someone else's food who cannot afford it. It is being glad for others who get a promotion even when you did not. It is visiting those who are lonely. It is allowing others to get a better place in traffic without complaining. It is teaching what you know. It is being a gracious winner or loser. It is ignoring your rights to help others. It is not mocking others who are different. It is mowing a neighbor's yard when they can't. It is giving one of something when you have two. It is being brave enough to mention God to others. Be creative and find ways to love. And do it with the right attitude.

Anything we do for others should be balanced. We need to be perceptive enough to give what the real need is. Some people will abuse your kindness and love. You need to be discerning. If you have been abused, trust God, and avoid being abused again if you can help it. And, forgive and love the person.

The challenge Jesus has given us, when He said we are to be perfect, as God is perfect, takes more focus. The

Margin references:
John 13:34

1 Sam. 20:17

Song of Sol. 1:2

Rom. 13:9

challenge could properly be restated as to love others as God does. | Matt. 5:48

The song from The Beatles says "All you need is love…" It's amazing how accurate that is. Truly, that is all you need.

Verses from this section:

Matthew 22:36 "Teacher, which is the great commandment in the Law?"

Matthew 22:37 And he said to him, "You shall love the Lord your God with all your heart and with all your soul and with all your mind.

Matthew 22:38 This is the great and first commandment.

Matthew 22:39 And a second is like it: You shall love your neighbor as yourself.

Matthew 22:40 On these two commandments depend all the Law and the Prophets."

1 John 2:10 Whoever loves his brother abides in the light, and in him there is no cause for stumbling.

1 Peter 1:22 Having purified your souls by your obedience to the truth for a sincere brotherly love, love one another earnestly from a pure heart

1 Corinthians 13:4 Love is patient and kind; love does not envy or boast; it is not arrogant

1 Corinthians 13:5 or rude. It does not insist on its own way; it is not irritable or resentful;

1 Corinthians 13:6 it does not rejoice at wrongdoing, but rejoices with the truth.

1 Corinthians 13:7 Love bears all things, believes all things, hopes all things, endures all things.

Philippians 2:3-4 Do nothing from selfish ambition or conceit, but in humility count others more significant than yourselves. Let each of you look not only to his own interests, but also to the interests of others.

John 13:34 A new commandment I give to you, that you love one another: just as I have loved you, you also are to love one another.

1 Timothy 2:4 who desires all people to be saved and to come to the knowledge of the truth.

1 Samuel 20:17 And Jonathan made David swear again by his love for him, for he loved him as he loved his own soul.

Song 1:2 Let him kiss me with the kisses of his mouth! For your love is better than wine

Romans 13:9 For the commandments, "You shall not commit adultery, You shall not murder, You shall not steal, You shall not covet," and any other commandment, are summed up in this word: "You shall love your neighbor as yourself."

Matthew 5:48 You therefore must be perfect, as your heavenly Father is perfect.

17

TELL ME ABOUT THE END TIMES

Eternity is forever. It's difficult to grasp, because everything around us is temporary, and especially since the lifespan for people is relatively short. Eternity is endless, and our life here on earth is short. Yet, during our few years here on earth, our fate for all of eternity is set. It is important to become a Christian, to start a relationship with God through Jesus, because it sets our forever destiny. Christians will be with God forever. | Heb. 7:25 Matt. 25:46 Phil. 3:20

The alternative is to be away from God forever, in pain and torment. This is hell, and it is real. | Luke 16:23

Jesus came to earth long ago to offer Himself so we could be with God in heaven. At some point in the future, we know Jesus will return to earth. When He does, the manner in which He returns will be very different from the way He left. He will come with great fanfare. We will hear the voices of angels and the trumpets of God. | John 19:30 Acts 7:59 Matt. 24:30 1 Thess. 4:16 Matt. 24:27

Will we know when the end times are near? There is one thing we can be certain of regarding end times—no one knows when it will take place, not even Jesus. Only God knows. There are general events mentioned in the Bible that signify the end times are approaching, but there are differences of opinion trying to map these events to current events. These are events like who will be ruling, what kinds of conflicts exist between nations, what types of rules will be in place across the world, and what kinds of weather patterns we will experience. | Mark 13:32 Matt. 24:7 Luke 21:11

There are a lot of opinions on the sequence of events at the end times as well. The most important things to know are that Jesus will return, and at some time after that the Universe and earth as we know it will be destroyed. A new heaven and earth will replace it. We will again have a physical body and mind, and will live on the new earth, but it will be vastly different. There will be no more death, | John 14:3 Luke 17:29-30 Matt. 24:35 2 Pet. 3:7 Rev. 21:1 Rev. 21:4

Rev. 21:27	and no more sin and the effects of sin. Because of that we will be in perfect peace and contentment.
Rev. 20:10	Satan and his fallen angels will be fully defeated, and in hell, in great torment and unable to influence anyone on the new earth.
Rom. 14:17 Gal. 5:22	We cannot truly comprehend what heaven or hell will be like, but we know enough. And one day we will know in great detail. We will see it, and live it. We will either find heaven far greater than we could imagine, or we will find hell far worse than we could imagine.
Rom. 14:10	At the end times, each person will face judgment. Those without faith in Jesus will be destined for hell. Those who trusted their lives to Jesus will be destined for heaven.
1 Cor. 3:13-14	For Christians, in the final judgment, we won't be punished for what we did wrong because Jesus' death covers that. We will be rewarded for what we did to help others. But there will be no comparing and jealousy among ourselves. We will fully enjoy each other's gains.
John 14:2-3	As Christians, God and Jesus even now are preparing our eventual home, and it is something we can look forward to with the greatest of expectations.

Verses from this section:

Hebrews 7:25 Consequently, he is able to save to the uttermost those who draw near to God through him, since he always lives to make intercession for them.

Matthew 25:46 And these will go away into eternal punishment, but the righteous into eternal life."

Philippians 3:20 But our citizenship is in heaven, and from it we await a Savior, the Lord Jesus Christ,

Luke 16:23 and in Hades, being in torment, he lifted up his eyes and saw Abraham far off and Lazarus at his side.

John 19:30 When Jesus had received the sour wine, he said, "It is finished," and he bowed his head and gave up his spirit.

Acts 7:59 And as they were stoning Stephen, he called out, "Lord Jesus, receive my spirit."

Matthew 24:30 Then will appear in heaven the sign of the Son of Man, and then all the tribes of the earth will mourn, and they will see the Son of Man coming on the clouds of heaven with power and great glory.

1 Thessalonians 4:16 For the Lord himself will descend from heaven with a cry of command, with the voice of an archangel, and with the sound of the trumpet of God. And the dead in Christ will rise first.

Matthew 24:27 For as the lightning comes from the east and shines as far as the west, so will be the coming of the Son of Man.

Mark 13:32 "But concerning that day or that hour, no one knows, not even the angels in heaven, nor the Son, but only the Father."

Matthew 24:7 For nation will rise against nation, and kingdom against kingdom, and there will be famines and earthquakes in various places.

Luke 21:11 There will be great earthquakes, and in various places famines and pestilences. And there will be terrors and great signs from heaven.

John 14:3 And if I go and prepare a place for you, I will come again and will take you to myself, that where I am you may be also.

Luke 17:29-30 but on the day when Lot went out from Sodom, fire and sulfur rained from heaven and destroyed them all—so will it be on the day when the Son of Man is revealed.

Matthew 24:35 Heaven and earth will pass away, but my words will not pass away.

2 Peter 3:7 But by the same word the heavens and earth that now exist are stored up for fire, being kept until the day of judgment and destruction of the ungodly.

Revelation 21:1 Then I saw a new heaven and a new earth, for the first heaven and the first earth had passed away, and the sea was no more.

Revelation 21:4 He will wipe away every tear from their eyes, and death shall be no more, neither shall there be mourning, nor crying, nor pain anymore, for the former things have passed away."

Revelation 21:27 But nothing unclean will ever enter it, nor anyone who does what is detestable or false, but only those who are written in the Lamb's book of life.

Revelation 20:10 and the devil who had deceived them was thrown into the lake of fire and sulfur where the beast and the false prophet were, and they will be tormented day and night forever and ever.

Romans 14:17 For the kingdom of God is not a matter of eating and drinking but of righteousness and peace and joy in the Holy Spirit.

Galatians 5:22 But the fruit of the Spirit is love, joy, peace, patience, kindness, goodness, faithfulness,

Romans 14:10 Why do you pass judgment on your brother? Or you, why do you despise your brother? For we will all stand before the judgment seat of God;

1 Corinthians 3:13-14 each one's work will become manifest, for the Day will disclose it, because it will be revealed by fire, and the fire will test what sort of work each one has done. If the work that anyone has built on the foundation survives, he will receive a reward.

John 14:2-3 In my Father's house are many rooms. If it were not so, would I have told you that I go to prepare a place for you? And if I go and prepare a place for you, I will come again and will take you to myself, that where I am you may be also.

18

SHOULD I TELL OTHERS ABOUT GOD?

God tells us He would like for every person to come to Him in repentance. His passion is for each person to come to Him, to believe and trust in Him, through Jesus. | 2 Pet. 3:9

Jesus, too, has that same passion. Before He left, He told His followers to go to all nations and make disciples, even to the remotest parts of the earth. | Mat 28:19-20 / Acts 1:8

We do need to tell others, otherwise they will lose that opportunity to choose between heaven and hell. They may have other opportunities, but that one will be lost. | Rom. 10:14 / Mark 16:15 / Matt. 10:7

If you could endlessly give a million dollars to other people, would you hesitate? That would be easy—every person would be thrilled and thank you. The gift of eternal life is worth much more than money. But it's difficult to grasp and to see its value. That is why faith is needed. Faith is being sure about something we cannot see. | Matt. 16:26 / Heb. 11:6

Nowadays there is a lot of negative views of Christians and Christianity, and people are not willing to listen. In so doing, they are missing out on the answers to the deepest questions people can have. The biggest challenge is how do you show others what a significant life you can have now and will have for eternity? How do you show them it is something they desperately need? | John 15:5 / John 6:51 / 2 Tim. 4:18

The best way to draw people to Christ is to appreciate them and help them as they need it. When you talk religion, don't sell. Show them your life, tell them what God has done in yours, and tell them what you know about God. | Eph. 4:32 / Rom. 15:1-2 / 2 Cor. 5:17

There are a lot of advantages and benefits to having a relationship with God, But the number one reason people need to come to God is not what they can get out of it. It is because the bullseye of life is loving and serving God. It is truth. It is the purpose for everything. | Ps. 119:160 / Luke 1:1,4 / Luke 4:43 / Acts 20:27

As a Christian, drawing people to Christ should be part of our life. We know it should be, but whether you are a new Christian, or have been one a long time, it is a tough challenge. Don't wonder why you struggle so much with this. We all do.

Acts 8:29-30

When others see your true heart in caring for them, they will want to listen. Even if you have just met someone, they should see you are talking with them about Jesus because you want good things for them. Teaching people you know is typically easier than talking with people you don't know, but many make the effort to talk to others they run into, like on the beach, in a mall, or in the city.

When you make the effort, you will see that there are fewer things in life more joyous than helping someone start a relationship with Christ.

Luke 15:7

Verses from this section:

2 Peter 3:9 The Lord is not slow to fulfill his promise as some count slowness, but is patient toward you, not wishing that any should perish, but that all should reach repentance.

Matthew 28:19-20 Go therefore and make disciples of all nations, baptizing them in the name of the Father and of the Son and of the Holy Spirit, teaching them to observe all that I have commanded you. And behold, I am with you always, to the end of the age."

Acts 1:8 But you will receive power when the Holy Spirit has come upon you, and you will be my witnesses in Jerusalem and in all Judea and Samaria, and to the end of the earth."

Romans 10:14 How then will they call on him in whom they have not believed? And how are they to believe in him of whom they have never heard? And how are they to hear without someone preaching?

Mark 16:15 And he said to them, "Go into all the world and proclaim the gospel to the whole creation.

Matthew 10:7 And proclaim as you go, saying, 'The kingdom of heaven is at hand.'

Matthew 16:26 For what will it profit a man if he gains the whole world and forfeits his soul? Or what shall a man give in return for his soul?

Hebrews 11:6 And without faith it is impossible to please him, for whoever would draw near to God must believe that he exists and that he rewards those who seek him.

John 15:5 I am the vine; you are the branches. Whoever abides in me and I in him, he it is that bears much fruit, for apart from me you can do nothing.

John 6:51 I am the living bread that came down from heaven. If anyone eats of this bread, he will live forever. And the bread that I will give for the life of the world is my flesh."

2 Timothy 4:18 The Lord will rescue me from every evil deed and bring me safely into his heavenly kingdom. To him be the glory forever and ever. Amen.

Ephesians 4:32 Be kind to one another, tenderhearted, forgiving one another, as God in Christ forgave you.

Romans 15:1-2 We who are strong have an obligation to bear with the failings of the weak, and not to please ourselves. Let each of us please his neighbor for his good, to build him up.

2 Corinthians 5:17 Therefore, if anyone is in Christ, he is a new creation. The old has passed away; behold, the new has come.

Psalm 119:160 The sum of your word is truth, and every one of your righteous rules endures forever.

Luke 1:1 Inasmuch as many have undertaken to compile a narrative of the things that have been accomplished among us,

Luke 1:4 that you may have certainty concerning the things you have been taught.

Luke 4:43 but he said to them, "I must preach the good news of the kingdom of God to the other towns as well; for I was sent for this purpose."

Acts 20:27 for I did not shrink from declaring to you the whole counsel of God.

Acts 8:29-30 And the Spirit said to Philip, "Go over and join this chariot." So Philip ran to him and heard him reading Isaiah the prophet and asked, "Do you understand what you are reading?"

Luke 15:7 Just so, I tell you, there will be more joy in heaven over one sinner who repents than over ninety-nine righteous persons who need no repentance.

19

WHY DO BAD THINGS HAPPEN?

Look at the good things that have happened in your life. Look at the bad things that have happened in your life. What is the difference? Why do you set certain events as good, and others as bad? And these bad events, why do we sometimes find them happening to good people? This is a basic question people looking at Christianity have, and one new Christians often ask.

Life is very complex. Each turn of events has many current and future affects related to it. There are certain events where there is no question whether it is good or bad, but for many events, tagging them as 'good' or 'bad' may be too simplistic.

How does God view these events? Look at the different ways in how a parent and a child see things. Many things both parent and child will agree on, but there are things they won't agree on. For example, when the child loses a friend who causes trouble, or when a neighbor requires payment for something the child broke, or when a child is getting puffed up about a certain skill and gets beat in a competition. It's obvious there may be good and bad in each situation. How you view it depends on how the event affects you.

Let's step back and ask again, how does God view events? Consider what God's priorities are. Number one on God's list is our relationship with Him. God is always working circumstances to draw us to Him. If the result of a circumstance is we get to know Him, or we are now closer to Him, then God sees that as a win.

The second priority for God is our character. God has a tremendous desire for us to have the nature of Jesus. We are to imitate Him in every way. But our sin nature greatly distracts us. Our character wanders all over the place. We are both noble and debased. We push forward to be more

Prov. 22:6
Eph. 6:4
Ps. 78:5

Heb. 12:11

Luke 15:10
John 3:16
1 Pet. 3:18
Ps. 145:18

Lev. 20:26
Matt. 5:48
Rom. 3:23
James 3:9-10

like Jesus, knowing we are not where we ought to be, but we have moved forward from where we used to be. God places things in our way to build us into who we need to be. Sometimes it only takes a minor adjustment (figuratively just a toothpick), but sometimes He needs to (figuratively) hit us over the head with a two-by-four. | Heb. 12:1

Heb. 12:11

Third on God's priority is giving us pleasant things. God loves to give us the desires of our heart—but only if they align with His first two priorities. | Ps. 37:4 / John 15:7

Our problem is we typically have those priorities upside down. What is our number one priority? We want pleasant things. We want things that help us have a good life. We often will neglect things that matter most to God so we can live in pleasant circumstances.

Be careful about trying to label an event with why it happened. Why did this "bad" thing happen? There could be hundreds of reasons for an event. And yes, there could be an overarching single reason for an event, but many times that is not the case. | James 1:2-3

There are very puzzling verses that tell us "in everything give thanks." Everything? How can we thank God in every situation? We can and should because God is working in every situation. He does not cause many of the "bad" things we experience, but He will work in every situation. Trust God. | 1 Thess. 5:18 / Eph. 5:20 / Rom. 8:28

A huge problem we have in this world is sin. We are all sinners, and sin is rampant. This also means the effects of sin are rampant. We see it in the news when we read or hear of terrible tragedies. And still, God will work in those situations. It is challenging, but we need to trust God in everything that happens. You may have been the recipient of evil actions or a tragic accident. But you need to find a way to use those to draw closer to God, to see how He can take those bad things and work good things in them. | Isa. 25:4 / John 16:33 / James 4:8 / Ps. 145:18

Sin always has consequences. Yes, sin in others' lives affects us, but we need to wake up to the fact that sin in our lives has consequences, even though we often think we have escaped from it. You may think you've been able to hide your sin, but the effects from that sin are having an effect on your life. | Prov. 29:6 / Prov. 12:21 / Isa. 57:21

Regardless, God will work in every situation. Trust God. He is merciful, He is forgiving, and He will work | Matt. 7:11

	with you to pick up the pieces. Examine your life. If there
Jer. 29:11	is sin, turn away from it, admit it to God, and ask for His
Deut. 7:9	guidance to avoid it.

with you to pick up the pieces. Examine your life. If there is sin, turn away from it, admit it to God, and ask for His guidance to avoid it.

The next time you find yourself in a bad circumstance, take a look at it from God's perspective. How is your relationship with Him? What have you been struggling with? Where is God taking you? How has your time with Him been lately? How has your prayer life been? We won't be able to understand the reasons for everything that happens to us because not everything will make sense. But draw close to God, trust Him in those events, and grow as a result. Build your relationship with God. Build your godly character.

Jer. 29:11
Deut. 7:9

Josh. 1:9
Ps. 9:10

Ps. 20:7

Verses from this section:

Proverbs 22:6 Train up a child in the way he should go; even when he is old he will not depart from it.

Ephesians 6:4 Fathers, do not provoke your children to anger, but bring them up in the discipline and instruction of the Lord.

Psalm 78:5 He established a testimony in Jacob and appointed a law in Israel, which he commanded our fathers to teach to their children

Hebrews 12:11 For the moment all discipline seems painful rather than pleasant, but later it yields the peaceful fruit of righteousness to those who have been trained by it.

Luke 15:10 Just so, I tell you, there is joy before the angels of God over one sinner who repents."

John 3:16 "For God so loved the world, that he gave his only Son, that whoever believes in him should not perish but have eternal life.

1 Peter 3:18 For Christ also suffered once for sins, the righteous for the unrighteous, that he might bring us to God, being put to death in the flesh but made alive in the spirit,

Psalm 145:18 The Lord is near to all who call on him, to all who call on him in truth.

Leviticus 20:26 You shall be holy to me, for I the Lord am holy and have separated you from the peoples, that you should be mine.

Matthew 5:48 You therefore must be perfect, as your heavenly Father is perfect.

Romans 3:23 for all have sinned and fall short of the glory of God,

James 3:9-10 With it we bless our Lord and Father, and with it we curse people who are made in the likeness of God. From the same mouth come blessing and cursing. My brothers, these things ought not to be so.

Hebrews 12:1 Therefore, since we are surrounded by so great a cloud of witnesses, let us also lay aside every weight, and sin which clings so closely, and let us run with endurance the race that is set before us,

Hebrews 12:11 For the moment all discipline seems painful rather than pleasant, but later it yields the peaceful fruit of righteousness to those who have been trained by it.

Psalm 37:4 Delight yourself in the Lord, and he will give you the desires of your heart.

John 15:7 If you abide in me, and my words abide in you, ask whatever you wish, and it will be done for you.

James 1:2-3 Count it all joy, my brothers, when you meet trials of various kinds, for you know that the testing of your faith produces steadfastness.

1 Thessalonians 5:18 give thanks in all circumstances; for this is the will of God in Christ Jesus for you.

Ephesians 5:20 giving thanks always and for everything to God the Father in the name of our Lord Jesus Christ,

Romans 8:28 And we know that for those who love God all things work together for good, for those who are called according to his purpose.

Isaiah 25:4 or you have been a stronghold to the poor, a stronghold to the needy in his distress, a shelter from the storm and a shade from the heat; for the breath of the ruthless is like a storm against a wall

John 16:33 "I have said these things to you, that in me you may have peace. In the world you will have tribulation. But take heart; I have overcome the world."

James 4:8 Draw near to God, and he will draw near to you. Cleanse your hands, you sinners, and purify your hearts, you double-minded.

Psalm 145:18 The Lord is near to all who call on him, to all who call on him in truth

Proverbs 29:6 An evil man is ensnared in his transgression, but a righteous man sings and rejoices.

Proverbs 12:21 No ill befalls the righteous, but the wicked are filled with trouble.

Isaiah 57:21 "There is no peace," says my God, "for the wicked."

Matthew 7:11 If you then, who are evil, know how to give good gifts to your children, how much more will your Father who is in heaven give good things to those who ask him!

Jeremiah 29:11 For I know the plans I have for you, declares the Lord, plans for welfare and not for evil, to give you a future and a hope.

Deuteronomy 7:9 Know therefore that the Lord your God is God, the faithful God who keeps covenant and steadfast love with those who love him and keep his commandments, to a thousand generations

Joshua 1:9 "Have I not commanded you? Be strong and courageous. Do not be frightened, and do not be dismayed, for the Lord your God is with you wherever you go."

Psalm 9:10 And those who know your name put their trust in you, for you, O Lord, have not forsaken those who seek you.

Psalm 20:7 Some trust in chariots and some in horses, but we trust in the name of the Lord our God.

20

WHAT IS CHRISTIAN MATURITY?

When you decide to take up the game of golf, there are a lot of different ways of learning it. You can casually watch it on TV, and then go onto the golf course and give it a try. You can go to the driving range, and practice, and then give it a try. Or you could take lessons, study the game, and practice often. It really depends on what you want to get out of the game, and what your goals are.

When you become a Christian, you have not only set your eternal destiny, but you have changed your life on earth. Where you go in life depends on how you approach the Christian life, and what your goals are. You can casually watch sermons in church, and go out and give it a try. Or, if you want more out of life, you can spend some time to understand what it should mean to live as a Christian, and take steps to accomplish that.

It is important to note that where you go in your Christian life is where you will go in life. Look at what life is—a creation by God, watched and prodded and loved by God. At first, He wants to have a relationship with you. And, when you become a Christian, He then watches you travel through life, living with and following Him. This is what life is all about.

Living with and following God... how does one go about doing this? Simple. Spend time with God, and learn how He wants you to live, and do it. God does not want you to stay as an infant in the Christian walk, but to grow and mature. The more you spend time with God in prayer and reading the Bible, the more you will understand what Christian maturity is, and the more it will become part of your life.

The more you comprehend what it means to be a mature Christian, and the more it becomes a part of you,

2 Cor. 5:17
Gal. 2:20

Col. 2:6
1 Cor. 13:11
Matt. 13:23

1 John 4:13
2 Cor. 3:18

Matt. 5:48
1 Pet. 2:2
2 Tim. 3:16-17
James 1:4

	the more success you will have in life. God will honor this, and you will be blessed and the richer your life will be.
Eph. 4:13-15	

Oddly, the key to this success, to these blessings for you, is to take the focus off you. Focus instead on God and others. This isn't just a trite saying—this is a universal truth. You will see it throughout Scripture.

Phil. 2:3-4

Here is a list of some of the traits of a mature Christian. Notice where the focus is.

1 Cor. 10:33
- You have a good reputation—people know your character, and they talk good of you

1 Tim. 3:2-9
- You make the effort to live the way God wants you to
- People feel comfortable around you

1 Pet. 2:1-3
- You spend time with God in prayer and studying the Bible

Col. 1:28
- You have grown to where you can teach others to do the same
- You deal gently and peaceably with others
- You talk well of others—your speech is gracious, kind
- You forgive others

Matt. 6:14-15
- You have self-control in spending, lusts, drinking, and any other areas that would distract you from God
- You are hospitable—this doesn't just mean your home is comfortable, but you take care of people, and they are comfortable around you

Rom. 3:23
Rom. 7:15
1 Cor. 11:1

All people struggle with sin, with not doing what God wants. So how can you ever hope to have a good relationship with God when you still sin? Even Paul, in the Bible, admitted to his great struggle with sin, saying he still winds up doing the very things he hates. Yet he also tells others to imitate him.

John 17:6
Job 1:1

Near the end of Jesus' time on earth, He says of the apostles who had been with Him for three years, "They have kept your word." Amazing—they were still sinners, regularly failing, yet Jesus makes this statement about them.

And what about new Christians? How can they ever hope to act the way God wants, after years of following the wrong paths? What does God expect?

Here is what God is looking for in you—He wants to see progress. He wants to see that you have a passion for Him, and that you want what He wants for you. He wants to see you working in that direction, so you can regularly say, "I'm not yet where I need to be, but I'm not where I used to be." It comes down to, how are you living your life? Are you seeking to spend time with God, seeking to learn what He would have you do, and trying to do it? | Mic. 6:8
Phil. 3:12-14

Be careful not to compare yourself to others, to their growth or maturity. A new golfer cannot golf like a pro, and certainly should not get frustrated because they cannot. In your Christian walk, instead of getting frustrated, watch those you respect, who have some of the maturity you seek, and learn from and copy them. And practice it, so it becomes part of you. | Phil. 3:17
2 Thess. 3:7
1 Cor. 11:1
Heb. 5:14

We are encouraged to push forward as if we are running a race. We are to lay to the side the things that slow us down (like sin), and run with endurance, focusing on Jesus as we go. As an athlete pushes hard to win, so should we, not accepting mediocrity. | Heb. 12:1-2
1 Cor. 9:24-27

The greatest life you can live is one where you live in a close relationship with God, working with Him to grow in the faith, maturing as you go. Thus, one day you will be able to say as Paul did, "I have fought the good fight, I have finished the race, I have kept the faith." | Acts 20:24
2 Tim. 4:7
2 Cor. 13:9
Phil. 1:6
2 Cor. 8:11

Are you ready to run the race? Each day ask "God, I'm ready. What do You have for me to do today?" | John 17:4

Verses from this section:

2 Corinthians 5:17 Therefore, if anyone is in Christ, he is a new creation. The old has passed away; behold, the new has come.

Galatians 2:20 I have been crucified with Christ. It is no longer I who live, but Christ who lives in me. And the life I now live in the flesh I live by faith in the Son of God, who loved me and gave himself for me.

Colossians 2:6 Therefore, as you received Christ Jesus the Lord, so walk in him,

1 Corinthians 13:11 When I was a child, I spoke like a child, I thought like a child, I reasoned like a child. When I became a man, I gave up childish ways.

Matthew 13:23 As for what was sown on good soil, this is the one who hears the word and understands it. He indeed bears fruit and yields, in one case a hundredfold, in another sixty, and in another thirty."

1 John 4:13 By this we know that we abide in him and he in us, because he has given us of his Spirit.

2 Corinthians 3:18 And we all, with unveiled face, beholding the glory of the Lord, are being transformed into the same image from one degree of glory to another. For this comes from the Lord who is the Spirit.

Matthew 5:48 You therefore must be perfect, as your heavenly Father is perfect.

1 Peter 2:2 Like newborn infants, long for the pure spiritual milk, that by it you may grow up into salvation—

2 Timothy 3:16-17 All Scripture is breathed out by God and profitable for teaching, for reproof, for correction, and for training in righteousness, that the man of God may be complete, equipped for every good work.

James 1:4 And let steadfastness have its full effect, that you may be perfect and complete, lacking in nothing.

Ephesians 4:13 until we all attain to the unity of the faith and of the knowledge of the Son of God, to mature manhood, to the measure of the stature of the fullness of Christ,

Ephesians 4:14 so that we may no longer be children, tossed to and fro by the waves and carried about by every wind of doctrine, by human cunning, by craftiness in deceitful schemes.

Ephesians 4:15 Rather, speaking the truth in love, we are to grow up in every way into him who is the head, into Christ,

Philippians 2:3-4 Do nothing from selfish ambition or conceit, but in humility count others more significant than yourselves. Let each of you look not only to his own interests, but also to the interests of others.

1 Corinthians 10:33 just as I try to please everyone in everything I do, not seeking my own advantage, but that of many, that they may be saved.

1 Timothy 3:2 Therefore an overseer must be above reproach, the husband of one wife, sober-minded, self-controlled, respectable, hospitable, able to teach,

1 Timothy 3:3 not a drunkard, not violent but gentle, not quarrelsome, not a lover of money.

1 Timothy 3:4 He must manage his own household well, with all dignity keeping his children submissive,

1 Timothy 3:5 for if someone does not know how to manage his own household, how will he care for God's church?

1 Timothy 3:6 He must not be a recent convert, or he may become puffed up with conceit and fall into the condemnation of the devil.

1 Timothy 3:7 Moreover, he must be well thought of by outsiders, so that he may not fall into disgrace, into a snare of the devil.

1 Timothy 3:8 Deacons likewise must be dignified, not double-tongued, not addicted to much wine, not greedy for dishonest gain.

1 Timothy 3:9 They must hold the mystery of the faith with a clear conscience.

1 Peter 2:1 So put away all malice and all deceit and hypocrisy and envy and all slander.

1 Peter 2:2 Like newborn infants, long for the pure spiritual milk, that by it you may grow up into salvation—

1 Peter 2:3 if indeed you have tasted that the Lord is good.

Colossians 1:28 Him we proclaim, warning everyone and teaching everyone with all wisdom, that we may present everyone mature in Christ.

Matthew 6:14-15 For if you forgive others their trespasses, your heavenly Father will also forgive you, but if you do not forgive others their trespasses, neither will your Father forgive your trespasses.

Romans 3:23 for all have sinned and fall short of the glory of God,

Romans 7:15 For I do not understand my own actions. For I do not do what I want, but I do the very thing I hate.

1 Corinthians 11:1 Be imitators of me, as I am of Christ.

John 17:6 "I have manifested your name to the people whom you gave me out of the world. Yours they were, and you gave them to me, and they have kept your word.

Job 1:1 There was a man in the land of Uz whose name was Job, and that man was blameless and upright, one who feared God and turned away from evil.

Micah 6:8 He has told you, O man, what is good; and what does the Lord require of you but to do justice, and to love kindness, and to walk humbly with your God?

Philippians 3:12 Not that I have already obtained this or am already perfect, but I press on to make it my own, because Christ Jesus has made me his own.

Philippians 3:13 Brothers, I do not consider that I have made it my own. But one thing I do: forgetting what lies behind and straining forward to what lies ahead,

Philippians 3:14 I press on toward the goal for the prize of the upward call of God in Christ Jesus.

Philippians 3:17 Brothers, join in imitating me, and keep your eyes on those who walk according to the example you have in us.

2 Thessalonians 3:7 For you yourselves know how you ought to imitate us, because we were not idle when we were with you,

1 Corinthians 11:1 Be imitators of me, as I am of Christ.

Hebrews 5:14 But solid food is for the mature, for those who have their powers of discernment trained by constant practice to distinguish good from evil.

Hebrews 12:1-2 Therefore, since we are surrounded by so great a cloud of witnesses, let us also lay aside every weight, and sin which clings so closely, and let us run with endurance the race that is set before us, looking to Jesus, the founder and perfecter of our faith, who for the joy that was set before him endured the cross, despising the shame, and is seated at the right hand of the throne of God.

1 Corinthians 9:24 Do you not know that in a race all the runners run, but only one receives the prize? So run that you may obtain it.

1 Corinthians 9:25 Every athlete exercises self-control in all things. They do it to receive a perishable wreath, but we an imperishable.

1 Corinthians 9:26 So I do not run aimlessly; I do not box as one beating the air.

1 Corinthians 9:27 But I discipline my body and keep it under control, lest after preaching to others I myself should be disqualified.

Acts 20:24 But I do not account my life of any value nor as precious to myself, if only I may finish my course and the ministry that I received from the Lord Jesus, to testify to the gospel of the grace of God.

2 Timothy 4:7 I have fought the good fight, I have finished the race, I have kept the faith.

2 Corinthians 13:9 For we are glad when we are weak and you are strong. Your restoration is what we pray for.

Philippians 1:6 And I am sure of this, that he who began a good work in you will bring it to completion at the day of Jesus Christ.

2 Corinthians 8:11 So now finish doing it as well, so that your readiness in desiring it may be matched by your completing it out of what you have.

John 17:4 I glorified you on earth, having accomplished the work that you gave me to do.

21

HOW DO I STUDY THE BIBLE?

The more we know what the Bible says, the more we understand God, and the more we get to know Him. The Bible should become part of our thinking, teaching us how to view the world around us. — 2 Tim. 3:16-17 / Heb. 4:12

The first way we get to know the Bible is from what we hear from others, like in sermons and Bible studies. This is important and useful, but it's difficult to absorb and retain very much of what we hear. That is why we need to read the Bible ourselves. — 2 Tim. 1:13

Set aside a special time and place to read each day, to spend some private time with God. People tend to call this a Quiet Time. This is your time to pray and read, drawing closer to God. — Matt. 14:23

There are many ways to determine what to read. You can read through the Bible starting with Genesis, or follow a program that tells what to read each day, such as a small daily passage. Any program that gets you into the Bible each day is good. You have to find out what works best for you. — Ps. 119:131 / Ps. 119:105

Along with reading, to absorb more of what it means, you need to study it. There are many ways to do this, and here are some ideas: — Ezra 7:10

- Each day write down what you read and what it meant to you.

- Get a study book and work through it. These often have places where you can answer questions and write down thoughts. There are many study books available, for all levels.

- In each passage you read, answer Who, What, When, Why, How, for what you read.

- There are many commentaries on the Bible. These are books that explain each passage from the different perspective and learning of the authors. They will help you to understand some of the concepts that may not be obvious to you.

Ps. 119:11

To keep words of the Bible with you at all times, even when you do not have a Bible physically with you, you should memorize verses. Everyone can—it just takes time. Here's suggestions on how to do it:

- Write down each verse on a separate piece of paper, such as a three-by-five index card or a business card.

- Memorize in only one translation. You'll have less confusion over time.

- When reviewing the verse, say the verse reference, then the text of the verse, then say the reference again.

- Keep a collection of your verses, and regularly review them so you won't forget them.

Ps. 119:97
Phil. 4:8

Ps. 119:18

To get into the depths of verses, into the deepest meanings, you should meditate on the verse. Spend a lot of time on it. Pray God reveals something from the verse that He wants you to know. Examine each word, why it is there, what it implies, how it fits. Think about why God placed this verse in the Bible, and what He is trying to tell us.

Isa. 41:10

Before and after you read, pray about it. During your study, trust the Holy Spirit will speak to you in special ways. Listen to what He may be saying to you.

Matt 11:28
Ezek. 34:11
John 4:23

When you have set aside a time and place to study, know that God will be waiting for you each day, to enjoy His time with you.

Verses from this section:

2 Timothy 3:16-17 All Scripture is breathed out by God and profitable for teaching, for reproof, for correction, and for training in righteousness, that the man of God may be complete, equipped for every good work.

Hebrews 4:12 For the word of God is living and active, sharper than any two-edged sword, piercing to the division of soul and of spirit, of joints and of marrow, and discerning the thoughts and intentions of the heart.

2 Timothy 1:13 Follow the pattern of the sound words that you have heard from me, in the faith and love that are in Christ Jesus.

Matthew 14:23 And after he had dismissed the crowds, he went up on the mountain by himself to pray. When evening came, he was there alone,

Psalm 119:131 I open my mouth and pant, because I long for your commandments.

Psalm 119:105 Your word is a lamp to my feet and a light to my path.

Ezra 7:10 For Ezra had set his heart to study the Law of the Lord, and to do it and to teach his statutes and rules in Israel.

Psalm 119:11 I have stored up your word in my heart, that I might not sin against you.

Psalm 119:97 Oh how I love your law! It is my meditation all the day.

Philippians 4:8 Finally, brothers, whatever is true, whatever is honorable, whatever is just, whatever is pure, whatever is lovely, whatever is commendable, if there is any excellence, if there is anything worthy of praise, think about these things.

Psalm 119:18 Open my eyes, that I may behold wondrous things out of your law.

Isaiah 41:10 fear not, for I am with you; be not dismayed, for I am your God; I will strengthen you, I will help you, I will uphold you with my righteous right hand.

Matthew 11:28 Come to me, all who labor and are heavy laden, and I will give you rest.

Ezekiel 34:11 For thus says the Lord God: Behold, I, I myself will search for my sheep and will seek them out.

John 4:23 But the hour is coming, and is now here, when the true worshipers will worship the Father in spirit and truth, for the Father is seeking such people to worship him.

22

OTHER IMPORTANT TOPICS

I want to share a few other important things we find in the Bible.

Selflessness

Earlier, the chapter on Love told of how love is a summary of all the commandments. The most complete way to love and to treat people properly is to focus on them, not yourself. Oddly, you will get more out of life by wanting less for yourself. Earnestly work to ignore your own needs, so others can be blessed. And do it all the time, not just in moments of altruism.

Phil. 2:3-4

Jesus said He did not come to serve Himself, but to serve others. May this be the goal in our lives too. He said that he who wishes to lose his life will save it. Jesus meant this about how you give of yourself to others.

Mark 10:45
Luke 9:24

He asked us to take up our cross daily, meaning we should be willing to sacrifice. We should do for others not just when it's convenient, but also when it's tough.

Luke 9:23

Humility

Most people misunderstand what humility is. They picture humility in a person who has been humbled by people and life, who is quiet, often with little self-confidence, someone who even struggles to look you in the eye. This is a wrong view of humility.

Humility is a focal trait of a mature Christian. Humility is seeing yourself as God sees you, neither too low nor too high. Certainly if you think too much of yourself, that is not being humble. But those who think too little of themselves are also not humble—it is an inaccurate view of self, and not how God sees you. This is a form of selfishness because the focus is still on yourself.

1 Pet. 5:5-6
Luke 14:11

True humility is not thinking less of yourself, but thinking of yourself less.

We are told in the Bible that Moses was the most humble man on the earth. He certainly was not weak, but a powerful man. A mature Christian is not a weak person, but a humble person who is strong because they are confident in God's involvement in their life. Num. 12:3 2 Tim. 1:7 1 Cor. 10:33

Avoid comparing yourself with others—it is never healthy. To have a humble spirit, focus on God and others, and not on yourself.

Counsel

No matter how much we think we know, no matter how perceptive we think we are, we cannot know or see everything. We gain better decision-making when we get others involved in helping us see all the angles, and think about things in a different way. Prov. 11:14 Prov. 28:26

"The way of a fool is right in his own eyes, but a wise man is he who listens to counsel." Prov. 12:15

"Iron sharpens iron, so one man sharpens another." Prov. 27:17

Many of us tend to not ask for help, thinking we can do it on our own. We might be able to do it alone, but it won't be the same. The Bible tells us over and over it is a huge mistake not letting others help you. Asking for help is not a sign of weakness, but a sign of wisdom. This is why companies have the board of directors—to give wise counsel to the company's leadership. Prov. 4:13

When someone offers you advice or correction, how do you respond? Is your first reaction disdain for the other person, especially if they don't have a position or known skill to be able to offer? When advice is given with good intentions, you should consider it, determine if a change is needed, and make sure you thank the person—it is a courageous person who offers advice with good intentions. Prov. 19:20 Prov. 27:9

You can also be courageous in offering advice to others, with a good heart. Do it carefully, because advice and correction are hard to receive. You can be a blessing to them.

People want to help you. Ask others for advice, and listen to them. You will give them the blessing of helping you, and you'll be giving yourself a huge blessing. You will be wise.

Prov. 15:31-32

The Mirror

If you are out to dinner, and someone points out food stuck on your cheek, even though it might be awkward, you appreciate it, and you clean it. Better than talking all evening with that food stuck there.

When you are out shopping, and you happen to look at yourself in a mirror, if something is out of place, you fix it. Everyone does.

James 1:22-25

The words of God we hear or read or study are a mirror. They show us things that are out of place, that need to change. How often do we hear a sermon and know it is speaking to a need in our life.

Eph. 4:22-24
Romans 12:2

But our efforts in responding to these different kinds of mirrors are very different. Certainly we clean the food particle. And, there isn't a person who doesn't fix their appearance when it is found out of place. Yet, the mirror that shows a necessary change in our life is mostly ignored.

2 Cor. 5:17
Eph. 2:10
Ps. 51:10

Most people won't change unless something serious in life forces them to. May you be the person who looks in the mirror of God's word, sees a need in your life, and does something about it.

The Tongue

When is the last time you said something you regretted? When is the last time you said a lie, or something harsh or unkind? How much trouble the wrong words can do, and you can't bring them back.

James 3:2

Taming our tongue to say the right things the right way is a struggle for every person. The Bible tells us if we can control our tongue, we can control every area of our lives.

Eph. 4:29

God asks that no unwholesome word come out of our mouths. The only words we speak should be what blesses those around us. We are to meet the need of the moment with the things we say.

You salt your food to perfectly set the taste to what is

pleasant. The Bible tells us to do the same for our words—they should be placed into the air to create a pleasant environment. | Col. 4:6

Does this mean we cannot joke? We can. But, we are not to joke with coarse joking, with words that are not appropriate or hurtful. | Eph. 5:4 / Prov. 26:18-19

We won't conquer our tongue, but still, this is a goal for maturity in Christ. And the closer we get to it, the more we become a blessing to Christ and to those around us. | James 3:9-10

Contentment

Each of us has been born with certain traits, and then circumstances and life choices have given us our identities. As a result, some of us are tall and some are short. Some are heavy and some are thin. Some are strong and some are weak. Some are rich and some are poor. Some are healthy and some are sick. Some have curly hair and some have straight hair. Some are dark and some are light. Some have large families, and some do not. | Ps. 139:13-14 / Eph. 2:10

The ways we compare ourselves to others is seemingly endless. No matter who we are, we have a yearning for something else, something we see in other people.

It's okay to have goals in life, but we need to be careful. It is okay to want more and better, but not to an unhealthy degree.

We sometimes see how others are treated better than ourself or someone from our family. We get angry, and maybe even bitter. We see someone else's child get picked for the team or for the play. We see someone else get the promotion. We see someone else win the award. Somehow we require a balance in life, and it does not come. | Prov. 9:10 / Hab. 3:17-18

You will never be content if you think happiness is getting what you want. That is especially true if you are judging your situation compared to others. Contentment is taking a look at what you have and where you are and knowing it is good. | 1 Cor. 4:7

You need to be thankful for what God has given you. You need to be thankful where God has placed you. You need to be thankful for your current situation. You need to be prepared to be thankful for what life brings your | Eccles. 3:13 / James 1:17 / 1 Thess 5:18

118

Ps. 136:25

Phil. 4:11

way. Paul, even though he had been abused and was in jail, was able to say he had learned to be content in whatever situation he was in.

Like Paul discovered, a secret to contentment is to take your eyes off yourself and your situation, and to focus on the needs of others and how you can help them.

Another secret is to be overwhelmingly thankful— thank God for who you are and what you have.

The more you can be content with yourself and your situation, the more peace you will have.

Rights

If you make a list of what your rights are, what would you place on the list? Would it include your freedoms? Would it include what you can buy? Would it include how people should treat you? What about how doctors treat you? How your family treats you? Are these your rights?

Prov. 9:10

Let's take a different look at what you have in life. Try to look at everything in your life as a privilege. It is a privilege you are healthy, not a right. It is a privilege you have a home, food, money, clothes, a car, not a right. It is a privilege when people treat you well, not a right. It is a privilege that you can go through traffic without an accident, not a right. It is a privilege when your spouse is intimate with you, not a right.

Ps. 37:30

What do you have that you did not receive? Every single thing in life is a gift from God, even if you worked hard for it. Don't demand what you don't have, and thank God for what you do have. It is a great privilege.

Wisdom

James 3:17

Wisdom is a trait that universally everyone needs and wants. Without it, we hurt ourselves, and with it, life is so much better.

James 1:5
Prov. 1:7
Prov. 4:6

Wouldn't it be great to become wise? Or, at least, to grow in wisdom? The fear of the Lord is the beginning of wisdom. As we gain more knowledge of God, we learn more about what wisdom is.

What is wisdom? It is simply making decisions the same way God would. God is all-wise and all-knowing.

The wiser we are, the closer our decisions align with what God would decide.

To become wise, start by fearing God. The more time you study Him and spend time with Him, the more you understand His ways, and the better your decisions become. Wisdom is finding out what God likes and doesn't like, and doing it.

Get close to God. Become wise.

1 Cor. 1:25
James 3:17

Prov. 3:13

Verses from this section:

Philippians 2:3-4 Do nothing from selfish ambition or conceit, but in humility count others more significant than yourselves. Let each of you look not only to his own interests, but also to the interests of others.

Mark 10:45 For even the Son of Man came not to be served but to serve, and to give his life as a ransom for many."

Luke 9:24 For whoever would save his life will lose it, but whoever loses his life for my sake will save it.

Luke 9:23 And he said to all, "If anyone would come after me, let him deny himself and take up his cross daily and follow me.

1 Peter 5:5-6 Likewise, you who are younger, be subject to the elders. Clothe yourselves, all of you, with humility toward one another, for "God opposes the proud but gives grace to the humble." Humble yourselves, therefore, under the mighty hand of God so that at the proper time he may exalt you,

Luke 14:11 For everyone who exalts himself will be humbled, and he who humbles himself will be exalted."

Numbers 12:3 Now the man Moses was very meek, more than all people who were on the face of the earth.

2 Timothy 1:7 for God gave us a spirit not of fear but of power and love and self-control.

1 Corinthians 10:33 just as I try to please everyone in everything I do, not seeking my own advantage, but that of many, that they may be saved.

Proverbs 11:14 Where there is no guidance, a people falls, but in an abundance of counselors there is safety.

Proverbs 28:26 Whoever trusts in his own mind is a fool, but he who walks in wisdom will be delivered.

Proverbs 12:15 The way of a fool is right in his own eyes, but a wise man listens to advice.

Proverbs 27:17 Iron sharpens iron, and one man sharpens another.

Proverbs 4:13 Keep hold of instruction; do not let go; guard her, for she is your life.

Proverbs 19:20 Listen to advice and accept instruction, that you may gain wisdom in the future.

Proverbs 27:9 Oil and perfume make the heart glad, and the sweetness of a friend comes from his earnest counsel.

Proverbs 15:31-32 The ear that listens to life-giving reproof will dwell among the wise. Whoever ignores instruction despises himself, but he who listens to reproof gains intelligence.

James 1:22 But be doers of the word, and not hearers only, deceiving yourselves.

James 1:23 For if anyone is a hearer of the word and not a doer, he is like a man who looks intently at his natural face in a mirror.

James 1:24 For he looks at himself and goes away and at once forgets what he was like.

James 1:25 But the one who looks into the perfect law, the law of liberty, and perseveres, being no hearer who forgets but a doer who acts, he will be blessed in his doing.9

Ephesians 4:22-24 to put off your old self, which belongs to your former manner of life and is corrupt through deceitful desires, and to be renewed in the spirit of your minds, and to put on the new self, created after the likeness of God in true righteousness and holiness.

Romans 12:2 Do not be conformed to this world, but be transformed by the renewal of your mind, that by testing you may discern what is the will of God, what is good and acceptable and perfect.

2 Corinthians 5:17 Therefore, if anyone is in Christ, he is a new creation. The old has passed away; behold, the new has come.

Ephesians 2:10 For we are his workmanship, created in Christ Jesus for good works, which God prepared beforehand, that we should walk in them.

Psalm 51:10 Create in me a clean heart, O God, and renew a right spirit within me.

James 3:2 For we all stumble in many ways. And if anyone does not stumble in what he says, he is a perfect man, able also to bridle his whole body.

Ephesians 4:29 Let no corrupting talk come out of your mouths, but only such as is good for building up, as fits the occasion, that it may give grace to those who hear.

Colossians 4:6 Let your speech always be gracious, seasoned with salt, so that you may know how you ought to answer each person.

Ephesians 5:4 Let there be no filthiness nor foolish talk nor crude joking, which are out of place, but instead let there be thanksgiving.

Proverbs 26:18-19 Like a madman who throws firebrands, arrows, and death is the man who deceives his neighbor and says, "I am only joking!"

James 3:9-10 With it we bless our Lord and Father, and with it we curse people who are made in the likeness of God. From the same mouth come blessing and cursing. My brothers, these things ought not to be so.

Psalm 139:13-14 For you formed my inward parts; you knitted me together in my mother's womb. I praise you, for I am fearfully and wonderfully made. Wonderful are your works; my soul knows it very well.

Ephesians 2:10 For we are his workmanship, created in Christ Jesus for good works, which God prepared beforehand, that we should walk in them.

Proverbs 9:10 The fear of the Lord is the beginning of wisdom, and the knowledge of the Holy One is insight.

Habakkuk 3:17-18 Though the fig tree should not blossom, nor fruit be on the vines, the produce of the olive fail and the fields yield no food, the flock be cut off from the fold and there be no herd in the stalls, yet I will rejoice in the Lord; I will take joy in the God of my salvation.

1 Corinthians 4:7 For who sees anything different in you? What do you have that you did not receive? If then you received it, why do you boast as if you did not receive it?

Ecclesiastes 3:13 also that everyone should eat and drink and take pleasure in all his toil—this is God's gift to man.

James 1:17 Every good gift and every perfect gift is from above, coming down from the Father of lights with whom there is no variation or shadow due to change.

1 Thessalonians 5:18 give thanks in all circumstances; for this is the will of God in Christ Jesus for you.

Psalm 136:25 he who gives food to all flesh, for his steadfast love endures forever.

Philippians 4:11 Not that I am speaking of being in need, for I have learned in whatever situation I am to be content.

Proverbs 9:10 The fear of the Lord is the beginning of wisdom, and the knowledge of the Holy One is insight.

Psalm 37:30 The mouth of the righteous utters wisdom, and his tongue speaks justice.

James 3:17 But the wisdom from above is first pure, then peaceable, gentle, open to reason, full of mercy and good fruits, impartial and sincere.

James 1:5 If any of you lacks wisdom, let him ask God, who gives generously to all without reproach, and it will be given him.

Proverbs 1:7 The fear of the Lord is the beginning of knowledge; fools despise wisdom and instruction.

Proverbs 4:6 Do not forsake her, and she will keep you; love her, and she will guard you.

1 Corinthians 1:25 For the foolishness of God is wiser than men, and the weakness of God is stronger than men.

James 3:17 But the wisdom from above is first pure, then peaceable, gentle, open to reason, full of mercy and good fruits, impartial and sincere.

Proverbs 3:13 Blessed is the one who finds wisdom, and the one who gets understanding,

23

SOME FINAL THOUGHTS

There are many confusing things in this world, and it seems every person has a different view of truth. You can talk with anyone, and ask them questions about the universe, about the world around them, about life, about God, and about eternity. Guaranteed you'll get a different response from every person.

Yet, every person is unsure of the complete accuracy of their world view and would like to know what is the real truth, the ultimate truth, the correct view of reality. | John 14:6
There can only be one truth, but what is it?

We have been given a book that contains the perfect view of truth, put together by the author of truth, the | John 17:17
creator of the world. | Gen. 1:1

That book is the Bible.

There is another universal desire of people—to have peace. The true source of peace is with God through | John 14:27
Jesus. With God, through Jesus, you will have peace. Jesus | John 20:21
told us He has given us His peace—it was one of the things He said He would leave with us.

So we are given truth. And peace. What else is available to us from God through Jesus? Love, joy, | Gal. 5:22-23
patience, kindness, self-control, to name a few.

The closer we get to God, and the more we get to know Him, and the more we follow His ways, the more | Gal. 5:25
these things become a fundamental part of our lives.

When you go for a walk on a windy day, and you find | Acts 26:14
yourself walking against the wind, each step takes twice | Prov. 13:15
the effort. This is what life is like without Jesus. When you | Jer. 23:12
walk with the wind, it's as if you are floating along. This is | Rom. 8:28
what life is like with Jesus. | Ps. 17:5

Let me give you a challenge. Listed in this book are many of the benefits of knowing God and of living with God. When we make decisions, we weigh the benefits, the pros and cons. My challenge to you is to not see your decision to believe and follow God through Jesus as a decision you make because the benefits outweigh the costs. Make this decision because it is truth, it is correct, it is the way to live, it is walking with the wind.

Prov. 3:6
1 Tim. 1:17

Ps. 37:24

Living with God does not guarantee an absence troubles. Whether you walk against the wind or with the wind, when you pray, God hears you. If you pray right now, God will listen to you. To live with God, to walk with the wind when you haven't been, just change direction. Tell God you are sorry for your sins, you accept the gift Jesus gave you of forgiveness, and you want a relationship with God. We are able to do this because of what Jesus did—He opened up the door for us and offers this gift. If you do this, you are a Christian.

1 John 5:14

1 John 1:9
Rev. 3:20

Because you have become a new Christian, God will become very active in your life. New things will come, and old things will be put behind.

2 Cor. 5:17

One new thing is you should start to expect miracles. Do you believe God works miracles these days? A miracle is something that happened which would not have occurred had God not intervened. When we pray for things, and God did something that otherwise would not have happened, you need to realize a miracle took place. Every answer to prayer is a miracle.

Mic. 7:15
Matt. 15:31
1 John 5:14-15
Acts 26:18

Our prayer is that this book opens your eyes to the truths of God, and that you will have an understanding of the things of God which you never quite had before.

Eph. 1:18
2 Cor. 3:16

If that happened, you know what? It's an answer to prayer, and it's another miracle.

May you allow God to give you the life He has always wanted to give you. Amen.

Jer. 29:11

Verses from this section:

John 14:6 Jesus said to him, "I am the way, and the truth, and the life. No one comes to the Father except through me.

John 17:17 Sanctify them in the truth; your word is truth.

Genesis 1:1 In the beginning, God created the heavens and the earth.

John 14:27 Peace I leave with you; my peace I give to you. Not as the world gives do I give to you. Let not your hearts be troubled, neither let them be afraid.

John 20:21 Jesus said to them again, "Peace be with you. As the Father has sent me, even so I am sending you."

Galatians 5:22-23 But the fruit of the Spirit is love, joy, peace, patience, kindness, goodness, faithfulness, gentleness, self-control; against such things there is no law.

Galatians 5:25 If we live by the Spirit, let us also keep in step with the Spirit.

Acts 26:14 And when we had all fallen to the ground, I heard a voice saying to me in the Hebrew language, 'Saul, Saul, why are you persecuting me? It is hard for you to kick against the goads.'

Proverbs 13:15 Good sense wins favor, but the way of the treacherous is their ruin.

Jeremiah 23:12 Therefore their way shall be to them like slippery paths in the darkness, into which they shall be driven and fall, for I will bring disaster upon them in the year of their punishment, declares the Lord.

Romans 8:28 And we know that for those who love God all things work together for good, for those who are called according to his purpose.

Psalm 17:5 My steps have held fast to your paths; my feet have not slipped.

Proverbs 3:6 In all your ways acknowledge him, and he will make straight your paths.

1 Timothy 1:17 To the King of the ages, immortal, invisible, the only God, be honor and glory forever and ever. Amen.

Psalm 37:24 though he fall, he shall not be cast headlong, for the Lord upholds his hand.

1 John 5:14 And this is the confidence that we have toward him, that if we ask anything according to his will he hears us.

1 John 1:9 If we confess our sins, he is faithful and just to forgive us our sins and to cleanse us from all unrighteousness.

Revelation 3:20 Behold, I stand at the door and knock. If anyone hears my voice and opens the door, I will come in to him and eat with him, and he with me.

2 Corinthians 5:17 Therefore, if anyone is in Christ, he is a new creation.[a] The old has passed away; behold, the new has come.

Micah 7:15 As in the days when you came out of the land of Egypt, I will show them marvelous things.

Matthew 15:31 so that the crowd wondered, when they saw the mute speaking, the crippled healthy, the lame walking, and the blind seeing. And they glorified the God of Israel.

1 John 5:14-15 And this is the confidence that we have toward him, that if we ask anything according to his will he hears us. And if we know that he hears us in whatever we ask, we know that we have the requests that we have asked of him.

Acts 26:18 to open their eyes, so that they may turn from darkness to light and from the power of Satan to God, that they may receive forgiveness of sins and a place among those who are sanctified by faith in me.'

Ephesians 1:18 having the eyes of your hearts enlightened, that you may know what is the hope to which he has called you, what are the riches of his glorious inheritance in the saints,

2 Corinthians 3:16 But when one turns to the Lord, the veil is removed.

Jeremiah 29:11 For I know the plans I have for you, declares the Lord, plans for welfare and not for evil, to give you a future and a hope.

About the author

Scott Basham has spent nearly 25 years teaching Christians how to read and apply Scripture to their lives, focusing on building a strong foundation for life. Scott became a Christian as a teenager, and deepened his walk while attending the University of South Florida, where he obtained a mathematics degree. Soon after college, Scott married his wife Joy, and together they collaborated on helping believers in their walk. Scott began teaching Bible classes in 1992, and has taught people in a variety of life stages, including college age, men's groups, young marrieds, mid-life marrieds and senior adults. He and Joy have been happily married for over 37 years, and their three children are all grown and happily married. Each of their children have maintained a strong faith instilled in them by their parents. *Defining Christianity* is Scott's first book, and was developed from the years of teaching Biblical fundamentals.

Made in the USA
Columbia, SC
20 February 2019